Helping Bilingual Pupils to Access the Curriculum

Helping Bilingual Pupils to Access the Curriculum

GERI SMYTH

David Fulton Publishers
London

David Fulton Publishers Ltd
The Chiswick Centre, 414 Chiswick High Road, London W4 5TF

www.fultonpublishers.co.uk

David Fulton Publishers is a division of Granada Learning, part of the Granada Media
group.

British Library Cataloguing in Publication Data
A catalogue record for this book is available from the British Library.

ISBN 1–85346–876–2

Typeset by Mark Heslington, Scarborough, North Yorkshire
Printed and bound in Scotland by Scotprint, Haddington

Contents

Acknowledgements

My sincere thanks to the teachers and bilingual pupils of the schools where I undertook my doctoral research. The teachers' concerns and the pupils' experiences led directly to the writing of this book.

My thanks to colleagues in the Association for Teacher Education in Europe and the Scottish Association for Teaching English as an Additional Language who acted as sounding boards for the research presented here.

I would also like to acknowledge the contributions of past and present students at Strathclyde University Faculty of Education who trialled responses to many of the case studies and planning formats presented in this book.

Preface

This book was written as a direct result of research I undertook into mainstream teachers' responses to their bilingual pupils when they had little experience of working with such pupils, and little by way of policy support.

I have presented case studies of a number of the pupils and teachers I met during this research, and indicated the concerns of the teachers and the difficulties encountered by pupils when faced with an essentially monolingual curriculum. Suggestions are offered for meeting and overcoming these concerns and difficulties.

I hope that many teachers of bilingual pupils will be able to recognise their own concerns within these pages, and that the suggestions offered and the rationale presented will help them to overcome the challenges and enjoy the rewards of working with bilingual pupils.

CHAPTER 1

Language at Home/Language in the Classroom

This chapter begins with an overview of education and the linguistic make-up of schools in the United Kingdom (UK). The implications for teachers of a diverse linguistic make-up in their classes are investigated through a series of case studies drawn from research with mainstream teachers in primary schools. Educational policy for bilingual pupils in the UK is then discussed to help in understanding the diversity of response and the range of teacher concerns. These concerns are summarised at the end of the chapter and followed by a photocopiable set of questions to enable teachers to collect information about their pupils' linguistic, cultural and educational background. The chapter concludes with a set of targets for the teacher who has one or more bilingual children in the classroom.

Education in the UK

Education in the UK is compulsory between the ages of 5 and 16 years old. Children start school between the ages of 4½ and 5½ years old, attending primary school for six to seven years and secondary school for four to seven years. However, nursery education is available for all children from the age of 3 until they start school. The predominant model of teaching in British primary schools is one teacher per age-based class for all curricular areas for one school year. In secondary schools, pupils will usually be taught by a different teacher for each subject.

Since the 1950s increasing numbers of children being educated in the UK have been taught in English while their home language (i.e. the first language encountered at home) is other than English. Such children will be referred to throughout this book as bilingual, i.e. 'they use two or more languages in their everyday life' (Wiles 1985).

The linguistic make-up of the UK

Until the 1980s the large majority of bilingual pupils in British schools were located in inner-city schools. Usually second or third generation, these children were predominantly from a linguistic background originating from either the Asian sub-continent or Hong Kong. However, new patterns of immigration to the UK have resulted in pupils from widely disparate linguistic and cultural backgrounds being educated in schools across the country. Many of these schools have little or no history or experience of working with pupils from other than the dominant white, English-speaking background.

A range of factors has contributed to an increase in the number of home languages among pupils in British primary schools. Political changes worldwide (significantly, the opening of the borders of the former Eastern European Soviet bloc states and war in the former Yugoslavia) along with increased economic mobility (particularly within the member states of the European Union) have resulted in greater numbers of pupils who have European languages other than English as their first language. Increased inward investment from the Far East and the arrival of non-European postgraduate students and their families as universities compete to attract overseas students have added to the multilingual make-up of British primary schools. In Glasgow – one of the 32 unitary authorities in Scotland and one of the centres for dispersal of asylum seekers – there are now pupils with over 60 home languages, a pattern that is replicated across the UK.

Although there are still inner-city schools with large numbers of bilingual pupils and teaching staff specifically employed and qualified to support their needs, cuts in the education budget have reduced the number of specific support posts even in these schools. Increasingly, classroom teachers without specialist qualifications are being required to meet the needs of bilingual pupils without a coherent authority policy necessarily being in place in relation to the educational needs of these pupils, and with limited centralised support mechanisms.

How do teachers respond to the needs of their pupils in this context? The case studies in this chapter present some of the dilemmas faced by teachers with little or no experience of teaching children whose home language is not the language of the classroom. Subsequent chapters offer solutions to these dilemmas which will be familiar to many teachers who, like the teachers in these case studies, will be working in schools with small numbers of bilingual pupils.

MARY

Mary has been teaching for nearly 30 years. She has taught at most stages of the primary school but until recently had never taught a bilingual child. Mary is very committed to the needs of the children in her class. Two years ago Mai Ye, a

Cantonese-speaking girl, was enrolled in Mary's Year 1 class. This year Mary has found herself teaching Mai Ye's younger sister, Su Lin. This situation has led her to confront the reality that the girls use a language other than English in all but school contexts:

What really surprised all of us one day, Su Lin didn't have her gym things so I sent her along to find out if she could borrow Mai Ye's and she went in, asked the teacher obviously, and then started speaking in Cantonese. They didn't even you know [speak English] *to each other, outwith* [school] *. . . So I think at home there is no English spoken at all, they don't play with other* [English-speaking] *children.*

Dilemma

Mary had suddenly realised that the girls' preferred language for communication was a language about which she as a teacher knew very little. In the absence of a school policy to support bilingual learners, Mary was not being helped to build on this new understanding.

ELSIE

Elsie is a Year 4 class teacher with 20 years' experience in a number of primary schools in three different local authorities. She is a committed and successful teacher who has undertaken considerable continuous professional development. Elsie has never taught any children whose home language is other than English. Recently Chih Hai arrived in her class from Hong Kong. Chih Hai had no English language when he arrived in the school. Neither the school nor the authority have a policy or staff for supporting the needs of bilingual learners. Elsie has had to try to teach Chih Hai in a support vacuum. She is becoming increasingly concerned at the amount of individual attention she is giving Chih Hai without any apparent gains. Chih Hai has started behaving inappropriately in the classroom, shouting out and grabbing books and other resources from children in the class. Elsie recognises that Chih Hai's behaviour difficulties may have been caused by his frustrations at not being understood but she does not have any strategies for enabling Chih Hai to express himself in his first language:

I think that's what a lot of the problem was, his frustration at not being understood and no matter how hard I tried if he spoke to me in Chinese . . . I kept saying 'No, Mrs G not understand, not speak Chinese'.

Dilemma

Although Elsie expressed frustrations herself at not being able to understand Chih Hai, what she is ultimately expressing here is that it is the child's responsibility to be understood but this must be done in a way which conforms to school norms, i.e. in English.

Language education policy in the UK

In the context of many schools not themselves having detailed policies for the education of bilingual children, it is important to investigate exactly what is the official educational response to the needs of bilingual children. Societies respond to linguistic diversity in different ways (Malave and Duquette 1991; Baetens-Beardsmore 1993; Herriman and Burnaby 1996; Kaplan and Baldauf 1997). Educational responses to the needs of language minority children in the UK have evolved since the immigration from former British colonies in the 1950s.

Rattansi (1992) considers that language became a focus for educational responses to this evolving multicultural society in Britain with the publication of *English for Immigrants* (Department of Education and Science (DES) 1963). This was the first major government intervention into the teaching of children whose first language was not English. The language needs of the newly arrived immigrant population of schools were addressed in relation to the perceived need to ensure that their presence did not disrupt education for the white monolingual majority pupils. The cultural needs of the immigrant population were not addressed in official policy, a legacy that remains today.

Educational responses to the existence of children whose first language was not English have varied (Mills and Mills 1993) with initial responses to the education of bilingual children in Britain being focused on assimilation as quickly as possible into the so-called 'host community', ignoring children's specific language needs. As concern grew about the underachievement of ethnic minority pupils in British schools (DES 1985), responses developed into practices ranging from teaching bilingual pupils in separate language centres to withdrawing such children from their mainstream classes for the purposes of specialist English language tuition (Bourne 1990; Herriman and Burnaby 1996). This tuition often bore little or no relation to the child's curriculum in class and all these educational responses ignored the existence of the children's first language (Mills and Mills 1993).

Since the 1980s, the preferred approach has been to teach English language to children for whom it is an additional language in the context of other learning within the mainstream classroom (Wiles 1985; Scottish Consultative Council on the Curriculum (SCCC) 1994). This places demands on the classroom teacher to carefully consider the language needs of the bilingual child in relation to the content of classroom teaching.

Stubbs (1994: 207) argues that 'schools have always been the most powerful mechanism in assimilating minority children into mainstream cultures'. His analysis of the work of the committees which have produced statements on language in the education system for England and Wales concludes that this burgeoning of ad hoc language planning has created a 'sophisticated control which recognises ethnic diversity but confines it to the home, which pays lip-service to multilingualism but is empty liberal rhetoric' (1994: 207–8).

Thompson *et al.* (1996: 101) similarly suggest that UK government language policy may be discerned and analysed by considering the recommendations of official committees of enquiry into the education of speakers of languages other than English, or into the teaching of English in schools. Bourne (1990) provides a detailed historical overview of the changes in language policy as expressed in the Bullock Report (DES 1975), the Swann Report (DES 1985), the Harris Report (DES 1990) and the Cox Report (DES 1989), the latter resulting in the National Curriculum for English. These responses are particular to England and Wales, although all the named reports have had an influence on the situation in Scotland.

Bourne (1997: 85) stresses that in the changing context of British education, the support of bilingual children in mainstream schools requires a radical rethinking of policy. She is referring specifically to the effects in England and Wales of the 1988 Education Act, the National Curriculum and league tables, but her arguments apply equally to the evolution in Scotland of the 5–14 Curriculum Guidelines, National Testing, Best Value Assessment and Target Setting.

There is no language policy in the UK which states explicitly that home languages other than English should be eradicated, but neither is there an official policy document relating to the promotion of home languages. Language planning in Britain has been conducted by separate isolated committees with split consultation procedures (Stubbs 1994), different working groups having been responsible for developing guidelines for different areas of the curriculum.

A review of research into the achievements of ethnic minority pupils in England and Wales in the ten years following the Swann Report (DES 1985) was conducted by Gillborn and Gipps (1996). It is likely that their findings will be similarly if not exactly replicated elsewhere in the UK. Of particular concern is their finding that problems with language can sometimes be misinterpreted as indicative of deeper seated learning difficulties. This misinterpretation has resulted in inappropriate assessment or even exclusion from classroom life. Additionally, they found that negative stereotypes – particularly in respect to Asian communities – could lead to lower expectations for pupils.

The Scottish Council for Research in Education recently commissioned a review of research into educational issues affecting minority ethnic groups in Scotland (Powney *et al.* 1998). However, due to the isolated, small-scale nature of research in the area and the lack of detailed statistical information, the authors found themselves unable to answer the research questions set, including 'How does our [Scottish] educational system respond to the multicultural society it serves?'

In discussing the placement of children in mainstream education in Britain, Leung (1996) has identified the need for sound theoretical principles to underpin support for bilingual children in the mainstream classroom. Although placement practices for bilingual children differ throughout Britain, Leung's argument does apply across the boundaries of educational authorities.

Not only placement practices but also funding for and recording of the needs of bilingual children can vary considerably across different education authorities. Unlike the situation in England and Wales with Section 11 and Ethnic Minority Achievement Grant (EMAG) funding, there has never been separate allocation of funds to the education of bilingual children in Scotland. Some Scottish authorities still operate language support units, separate from mainstream schools, despite the Calderdale Report (Commission for Racial Equality (CRE) 1986) which argued that such withdrawal centres were in themselves racist: 'On the basis of current theory and research on second language acquisition, language withdrawal methods involving separate provision cannot be justified on educational grounds.' In England and Wales there is a diversity of uses of EMAG, including bilingual support, English as an Additional Language (EAL) provision, refugee pupils and African-Caribbean pupil achievement. This can lead to ethnic minority groups being pitted against each other in the bid for funds. This in turn can result in unhealthy and competing claims being made for the needs of refugee pupils versus permanent residents, and EAL versus mother-tongue support. In many authorities across the UK specialist EAL teachers are employed to help meet the needs of bilingual children. The deployment and remit of these teachers varies considerably, with many EAL teachers being employed on a peripatetic basis, having to respond to crisis when schools receive new bilingual pupils.

Constantino (1994) discusses the similarities and differences between the knowledge bases of mainstream and English as a Second Language (ESL) secondary teachers in the United States (US) concerning the theory and practice of bilingual education. In her interviews with six mainstream and five ESL teachers she found the mainstream, non-specialist teachers had very disparate opinions about language acquisition, resulting in the adoption of disparate practices in relation to the teaching of bilingual pupils.

Within the context of my research (Smyth 2001a) mainstream teachers' folk theories about the place of bilingualism in education were found to be similar across the sample. However, practices in my study were found to relate not only to the teachers' beliefs but also to what support systems for bilingual pupils were available in the different authorities. The absence of policy and the differentiated provision were found to be major factors in the adoption of disparate opinions and practices and, in some cases, lowered expectations of the bilingual pupils.

Constantino makes a direct connection between beliefs and practices, arguing that ESL teachers' understanding of language acquisition as a two-way process of negotiated input and output led them to utilise additional contextual support for the bilingual pupils, while the mainstream teachers – who had no clear beliefs about language acquisition – had lowered expectations of the bilingual pupils. This reflects the findings of Gillborn and Gipps (1996). Constantino, however, does not examine the reasoning behind teachers' beliefs, nor does she address practice in the context of a policy vacuum.

In order to investigate what informs teachers' practices, it is important to try to identify their beliefs about the needs of bilingual pupils. Work commissioned by the National Foundation for Educational Research (NFER) resulted in quantitative analysis of teacher attitudes to multicultural education (Brittan 1976). One of the findings of this research was that the majority of teachers did not believe that bilingual children would acquire a sufficient knowledge of English in mainstream classes alone, a belief that almost 30 years later may still hold power among mainstream teachers who have not been specifically taught how to address the needs of bilingual pupils.

At the start of the twenty-first century there is much political discussion within the UK about the need to ensure social inclusion at all levels of society. For schools this must involve the need to enable all children, regardless of their language background, to achieve their potential within the education system. A concern for social justice for all members of society must include a concern for those children who are educated in one language, English, and yet use another language as their main means of communication outside school. This enabling and inclusion undoubtedly presents non-specialist teachers with a number of queries about best practice for bilingual pupils.

The following two case studies will examine some of the more common concerns of mainstream teachers with regard to the education of their bilingual pupils in the context of limited knowledge and support. The chapter will conclude with a summary of teachers' concerns, which will then be addressed by subsequent chapters in the book.

ELSIE

In the previous case study we met Elsie and Chih Hai. As in many primary schools, homework in Chih Hai's class involves a book from the commercial reading scheme being sent home with pupils on a nightly basis. Elsie indicates on a bookmark the pages of the text to be practised for the following day. The expectation is that the parents will hear the child reading these pages aloud and sign the marker to indicate that this has been done satisfactorily. Some schools organise parental workshops on reading, but in many situations it is expected that knowledge will be transmitted between parents and from one generation to the next about home–school literacy practices. This is despite the work of researchers such as Taylor (1983), Heath (1983) and Kenner (1997) which has shown the diversity of home literacy practices and demonstrated the differences between home and school literacy practices.

Dilemma

In Chih Hai's case, his parents did not share this cultural knowledge about expected homework practices and so they required him to transcribe the text into the reading record. Elsie sought advice on how to resolve this dilemma:

Somebody at home is making him write it out, the pages you set. They are all written out. Not just once but he writes the sentence about four times. Should I not send it home? I mean that is the thing it would be nice to know. Am I doing the right thing?

Elsie later proposed the possibility of asking other Chinese adults, more fluent in English than Chih Hai's parents, to help with his reading in a way that more closely conformed with the expectations of the school.

Although she ultimately rejected this solution as 'imposing', what is important is that her proposal to seek help from a more competent English-speaker, rather than drawing on the linguistic and cultural competencies of the home, would have denied Chih Hai and his parents the opportunity to work together to help his literacy development because the school and parents did not share the same approach to reading.

KAREN

Karen is a Year 2 teacher with 13 years' teaching experience. Naser is a six-year-old boy in her class. Karen has taught bilingual children before but states that Naser is the first child she has taught who has presented her with any teaching dilemmas:

What his main trouble is really is lack of language. I don't think he's as – how shall I put it – not bright as he appears. I talked to his father at parents' night and I asked him how much English was spoken at home because his mother seems to speak Urdu all the time . . . he said not very much and I suggested that perhaps he spoke a lot more English in the house . . . he said that quite often he'd say something to Naser in English and he would look as if he didn't understand so he would repeat it in Urdu, which I said was fine . . . as long as he gets the English input.

Dilemma

In the interview extract just presented (and below), Karen substituted the word 'language' for English, placing no value on Naser's home language, as English was the only language which was recognised in the monolingual institutional context in which she was working. She considered it to be the parents' responsibility to enable Naser to become fluent in English and to fit into the school norms by speaking to him in English.

Karen has never before taught children who are not apparently fluent in English and she frequently wonders how much Naser understands in class:

I wonder how much he's taking in, I wonder how much of the language he gets . . . I always put it two or three different ways and even occasionally resort to pidgin English . . . just to make it as simple as possible.

Karen referred to using pidgin English to help Naser understand the language of the classroom. She believes in a common-sense view that language has to be simplified in order to be understood by foreigners and she applied this understanding to her interactions with Naser.

From the four case studies presented in this chapter we can see some of the common concerns and queries of mainstream teachers who find themselves teaching bilingual pupils when they have had little or no training as to how best to meet the needs of such learners.

Teachers' concerns

- What do you do as a teacher when you have no knowledge of a child's preferred language?
- How can you recognise the child's preferred language in your teaching when all the available resources are in English?
- How do you understand a child who communicates in a language you do not know?
- How do you communicate with parents when you do not share a language?
- How do you enable parents to support a child at home when the languages of the school and home are different?
- How do you know what a child understands in English when s/he produces little spoken or written English?
- What advice do you give parents about using English versus their home language?
- How do you modify your oral input to enable the child to understand you?
- **How do you do your best for this child?**

This final point has been highlighted because in all cases teachers' main concern for all children in their classroom is how they can best help the child to achieve his/her potential. The remainder of this book sets out to answer these questions for mainstream teachers by considering further case studies of classes, curriculum and children, and proposing solutions to the teaching dilemmas presented above.

An initial aid to resolving the teaching dilemmas which may be encountered when starting work with bilingual children is to gather relevant information about the pupil's linguistic, cultural and educational background, some of which may have been obtained by the school at enrolment. It is important that individual class teachers who are going to work with the pupil on a daily basis should have immediate access to this information. For this purpose there follows at the end of the chapter a photocopiable set of questions for teachers to complete with the aid of the child and his or her family.

Some school policies may prefer this information to be collected by the head teacher or a language or special needs coordinator (SENCO). However, there are benefits to be accrued from the information being collected by the teacher who will have most contact with the bilingual child. Not only will this ensure that the information is held by the person who needs daily access to it but also the process will be an important starting point for cooperation between parents and teacher in achieving **the best for the child**, identified earlier as the central concern of all teachers. Chapter 7 includes advice on writing a school policy for the education of bilingual pupils.

Once teachers have some of this basic information about the bilingual child's background they should set themselves some targets:

- Find written examples of the languages which the child sees and hears at home and display these in the classroom.
- Learn to say 'Hello' and 'Well done' in the child's home language.
- Try to incorporate the names the child uses for family members into stories you tell and contexts you set across the curriculum.
- If the child attended school in another country try to find out basic information about this educational system. For example, at what age do children start school? Are any languages studied other than the national language?

Further ideas will be found in Chapters 3 and 4 and resources to help with meeting these targets are listed at the end of the book (Useful Addresses and Websites).

Child's linguistic, cultural and educational background

CHILD AND FAMILY

Child's full name _____

How is this written in his or her home language?

_____

Child's preferred name for class use _____

For each person who lives in the house with the child (e.g. parents, siblings, other relatives) record what name the child uses for them at home:

mother	_____	father	_____
_____	_____	_____	_____
_____	_____	_____	_____
_____	_____	_____	_____
_____	_____	_____	_____
_____	_____	_____	_____

CHILD'S LANGUAGE USE

Which languages are used for oral communication in the home?

_____

In which languages is there written material in the home (e.g. newspapers, holy books, letters)?

_____

Which languages are listened to in the home for entertainment purposes (e.g. videos)?

_____

In which, if any, languages is the child literate?

_____

Child's linguistic, cultural and educational background

CHILD'S EDUCATION

What, where and for how long was the child's schooling before entering your class?

_____

Have there been any extended breaks in the child's schooling (e.g. for illness or travel purposes)?

_____

What were the child's preferences and/or dislikes in his or her previous education?

_____

CHILD'S CULTURAL BACKGROUND

Name of family religion (if any)_____

If the family religion involves formal worship when and where does this happen?

_____

Are there any dietary requirements associated with the religion?

_____

Are there any clothing requirements associated with the religion?

_____

What religious festivals do the family observe?

_____

CHAPTER 2

Meeting the Challenges of Teaching Bilingual Children

What does the research presented in Chapter 1 mean for the practising teacher with bilingual pupils in the classroom? The case studies in this chapter will analyse how children's home culture and bilingualism can be recognised and supported by monolingual teachers while enabling the children to achieve in a monolingual curriculum. Each of these case studies provides a picture of a bilingual child as defined in Chapter 1. Apart from their bilingualism the children are very different, demonstrating that there is no one answer to meeting the challenges of teaching bilingual children. The solutions need to be drawn from an understanding of the individual child, theories of bilingualism and pedagogical theory.

Each case study is followed by a discussion of the educational issues arising from it, the challenges for the teacher and some possible solutions to these challenges. It is hoped that although all the children present different challenges, teachers will find themselves familiar with some of these challenges and will therefore find the solutions useful in beginning to consider their own classroom practice. The case studies are followed by a proforma for teachers to address their own issues in relation to teaching bilingual children and a discussion as to how to resolve these issues.

JACK, AGE 9

Jack is in his fifth year of primary education in the UK. He was born in Scotland of a French mother and a Scottish father. He has been brought up bilingually, speaking French to his mother and English to his father. He attends French language classes on Saturday mornings and is as literate in French as his monolingual French cousin of the same age.

The class context

Jack's class has recently started learning French with two half-hour lessons per week given by the class teacher. She knows that Jack speaks French but not to what extent. As she is not a French specialist she is unsure how to differentiate the material which has been planned at authority level. After a few weeks, Jack switches off and makes no input in French classes.

Issues

Jack should not be taught in the French lessons in exactly the same way as his monolingual peers. His abilities in the target language need to be recognised, utilised and developed. This can present difficulties for non-specialist teachers who may be reluctant to isolate the child for special attention or may feel anxious about their own limitations in French.

Educational challenges

The teacher recognises that she is faced with a number of challenges by this situation:

- how to value Jack's French skills;
- how to make the French lessons meaningful for him;
- how to avoid isolating Jack in the classroom given his abilities.

Possible solutions

In a class lesson on, for example, colours, there are a number of opportunities for the teacher to respond to these challenges.

- Occasionally, it would be appropriate for Jack to act as a model for the French language. In order not to put pressure on Jack this could be done, for example, by asking him to be a quiz presenter. He could choose objects provided by the class teacher and ask the question: 'De quel couleur est le crayon?' This would be more advanced than the single word response of his peers. By giving Jack the opportunity to allot points to his peers for correct answers, he would have to listen to their responses and could also announce the scores in French.
- Jack and a partner could devise a colour poem. Both children could choose an item to describe by its colour, for example, 'Le soleil est orange' or 'Le ciel est bleu'. Jack could scribe the words and his partner could illustrate the

poem. This would allow Jack to use his French literacy skills and would prevent him having to work individually.

- The teacher stresses teaching language in the context of other classroom activities. Groups of children could mix paints to form new colours. Each group of children could choose their three favourite resultant colours and Jack could be asked to write labels for these new colours in French. This would challenge him to find the French equivalent for some more complicated words than the rest of the class might have been introduced to, for example, bleu marine etc. This would provide a purpose for Jack to use a bilingual dictionary.

OMAR, AGE 10

Omar is in his sixth year of primary education in the UK. He was born in England as were both his parents. His grandparents, who were born in Pakistan, also live with him. He speaks Punjabi at home to his grandparents. His parents want to maintain Urdu in the family, viewing it as a prestige language for their community. Omar's parents use Urdu to speak to Omar but he usually answers in English. His mother has taught him to read and write Urdu. He writes to his cousin in Pakistan in Urdu and he frequently watches Punjabi-language videos at home. Omar is also learning to read the Qur'an in Arabic at Mosque school.

The class context

Omar's teacher knows that English is not his first language but she does not know the name of the language he speaks. Nor does she know anything about his literacy in other languages. Omar appears to the teacher to understand the curriculum and to be fluent in spoken English. Recently the teacher has noticed that his written English appears to be rather stilted with a tendency to repeat taught ideas and little evidence of creativity in his writing.

Issues

It is not uncommon for bilingual children's apparent surface fluency in English to mask difficulties in using cognitive academic language. (See Cummins 1984 and 2000 for a discussion of this distinction. Chapter 5 of this text includes further discussion of the implications of this distinction for classroom practice.) These difficulties frequently only become apparent in the upper years of primary education when children engage in more independent writing tasks. In order for the teacher to be able to respond to her assessment of Omar's difficulties she needs to know more about his language background. This is a whole-school issue relating to communication with bilingual parents and to language monitoring. These aspects are discussed in Chapters 3 and 7. A possible format for language monitoring was provided in Chapter 1.

Educational challenges

The main challenges for Omar's teacher are:

- how to develop Omar's written English;
- how to acknowledge his linguistic strengths;
- how to avoid focusing on Omar's difficulties in written English as a learning deficit.

Possible solutions

Assuming she has been able to find out about Omar's language usage, there are a number of ways in which the teacher can begin to meet the challenges.

- Omar is already writing personal letters to his cousin in Urdu. He has the ability to be creative in his writing in Urdu but is not sure what is required of his writing in English as his home literacy has not provided models for this. By making the audience and purpose clearer to Omar he may be helped to produce more creative writing. The provision of writing frames (see Chapter 7) will help Omar overcome the repetitive nature of his writing while still providing a supportive model.
- The teacher is a firm believer in the importance of conferencing in the writing process but has so far had limited success with conferencing with Omar. Allowing Omar to write first in Urdu and then to talk in English to the teacher or a writing partner (see Chapters 6 and 7) about what he has written will help him to find suitable structure and vocabulary for writing in English.
- It is important that Omar's oracy and literacy in other languages are shared with and celebrated in the class and the school. The teacher could initiate a class Knowledge About Languages project with children finding and photographing examples of other languages and scripts in the local environment, for example, multilingual labels on food packages, menus from international restaurants, etc. More ideas for a Knowledge About Languages project can be found in Chapter 4.

ANNIE, AGE 7

Annie is in her second year of primary education in the UK. Annie and her parents are monolingual English-speakers. Annie's parents have decided that she should be educated in a Gaelic medium class as they firmly believe in maintenance of the Scottish culture, albeit Gaelic has never been part of their own heritage. They also know that the Gaelic medium classes tend to be smaller than the mainstream classes. They are very interested in Annie's education and regularly ask her about what she does in school. Annie usually replies 'nothing' or 'just the same'. Her parents are getting increasingly worried that they may have made the wrong decision in sending Annie to Gaelic medium education.

The class context

Annie is being educated in a Gaelic medium class within a mainstream primary school of which there are a number of models in place. In this class – where none of the children use Gaelic at home – there is Gaelic immersion for the first three years followed by a Gaelic-dominant bilingual phase. There is a national shortage of Gaelic medium teachers and the class teacher, while experienced in teaching and fluent in Gaelic, is new to Gaelic medium education. She is concerned that Annie and others in the class are not doing as well as she had hoped and she thinks this may be because the parents do not speak Gaelic.

Issues

There is a mismatch in the parents' and the teacher's perceptions of the difficulties here which goes beyond issues to be addressed in the classroom. In this situation the solutions are wider than whole school as there are implications for education authority language policy and teacher education. The teacher needs to become more aware of theories of second language acquisition (Skutnabb-Kangas 1981; Krashen 1982; Cummins 1984, 1986) and of learner differences (Ellis 1985) (these issues were discussed briefly in Chapter 1). However there are challenges that the teacher can address more immediately.

Educational challenges

The main immediate challenges for Annie's teacher are:

- how to involve Annie's parents in her education;
- how to develop the children's Gaelic language.

Possible solutions

- Annie's teacher is experienced with children and parents. In the past, as an English medium teacher, she organised parental workshops for the purposes of sharing the curriculum and resources. This can and should still be done. Although the resources are in a different language, the curriculum requirements and the methods are the same as in English medium education. This will reassure Annie's parents that there is no mystery to this educational medium and they will be able to support their daughter in her acquisition of new concepts.
- Annie and her classmates need a purpose for using their Gaelic outside the classroom. The rest of the children in the school are educated solely in English. Annie's teacher should arrange opportunities such as assemblies for the school community and story-sharing with the other classes which will allow the children to take their Gaelic outside the classroom. More ideas for sharing of languages can be found in the topic outlines in Chapter 4.

SUNITA, AGE 8

Sunita has just arrived in the UK from Somalia with her mother and younger brother, aged three. As an asylum-seeking family they have found themselves in an inner-city housing scheme as part of the Refugee Dispersal Programme. Sunita attended school intermittently over a period of a year before leaving Somalia. She speaks Somali and has begun to acquire literacy skills in Somali but has very little English language yet. Sunita's mother is very keen that she should attend school in the UK in order to continue her interrupted education.

The class context

Along with nine other asylum seekers of a similar age but different linguistic backgrounds, Sunita is taught in an in-school unit for refugee children. The educational emphasis is on English language acquisition. Sunita goes to a mainstream Year 4 class for art and physical education. She follows the other children's examples in these classes and seems competent and happy in both areas. However, she has not spoken to the class teacher yet. The school has not had any previous experience of working with children whose first language is not English. The teacher is very concerned as to how she will know that Sunita understands when she joins the mainstream class full time next term.

Issues

Sunita's teacher has to consider not only that she has little English at this stage but also the emotional implications of Sunita's past. Closs *et al.* (1999) indicated the importance of teachers and the school acknowledging and tackling the racism that many refugee families are experiencing in the UK, and preparing the other children in the school for the refugee children's arrival. The teacher needs to acknowledge that Sunita may understand English before she is ready to produce English orally or in writing. She must ensure that Sunita has plenty of meaningful opportunities to hear English and to practise it purposefully with her peers.

Educational challenges

The immediate challenges for Sunita's teacher are:

- how to help Sunita to feel part of the mainstream class;
- how to enable her to participate in an English language curriculum.

Possible solutions

- Before Sunita's arrival the teacher needs to help the class to understand what it means to be a refugee (see Rutter 1998). The teacher should then find buddies for Sunita who will help her in class, in the dining hall and in the playground. This should be more than one child to avoid an over-responsibility and to allow for absence and childhood squabbles.
- The teacher and the refugee unit need to liaise to discuss Sunita's learning styles and to arrange for further links prior to full mainstreaming during other curricular areas.
- The teacher frequently uses collaborative group work strategies across the curriculum as she believes this enables children's creativity. It is important to use this methodology as often as possible for Sunita to enable her to hear and use English other than from and with the teacher (see Chapter 7 for ideas for collaborative group work). This will also reduce the amount of individual time the teacher needs to spend with Sunita.

NATASHA, AGE 15

Natasha has been at school in the UK for two years and is now in Year 10 (3rd year) at secondary school. Her family came to Britain for work purposes. Both her parents are fluent in English and use English and Russian in their work. The family speak Russian at home. On her arrival in the school Natasha spent a few weeks in the school's language unit and was quickly moved to full-time mainstream education. She received EAL support once a week in English and history in Years 8 and 9 but having passed all her class tests at an average level and above, she was assessed as no longer requiring support. Having been at school for six years in Russia, she is literate in her first language and continues to read in Russian at home and to write to her friends in Russian.

The class context

In the English class the pupils are studying a unit on poetry: reading, writing and responding to a range of poems and poets. The class teacher has noticed that Natasha never volunteers a response and if she is asked a question directly or required to respond in writing to a poem, she tends to give very short, literal responses. The class has been studying *The Horses* by Edwin Muir and *Hawk Roosting* by Ted Hughes. The pupils are now required to write a poem in the style of one of the poets. Natasha is finding this very difficult and her work to date consists of single sentences on the theme of one of the poems.

Issues

As a result of subject assessments, the school has assumed that Natasha has had sufficient EAL support to make progress in mainstream certificate classes without further help. However, assessment which does not take account of the fact that English is not Natasha's first language is unlikely to give a complete account of her abilities in English. Poetic language is presenting new challenges for Natasha. She is unable to understand the figurative language of the poems being studied (*the tractors – look like dank sea monsters /the earth's face upward*) and therefore cannot use such language in her own writing.

Educational challenges

The teacher wishes to keep Natasha in the class as he believes she is intellectually capable of work at this level. The main challenges for the teacher are:

• how to enable Natasha to understand figurative language;

- how to enable Natasha to then use such language in her own writing;
- how to utilise Natasha's literacy in her first language in order to help her over-come these challenges.

Possible solutions

There are long-term solutions to be adopted by the school to aid Natasha and other bilingual pupils in addition to specific short-term solutions to be implemented by the class teacher.

- The school's assessment procedure needs to take account of pupils acquiring English as an additional language. Further discussion of what should be considered in respect of assessment in a policy for bilingual pupils can be found in Chapter 7. The Qualifications and Curriculum Authority (QCA) has produced valuable guidance on the assessment of pupils for whom English is an additional language (QCA 2000).
- For the purposes of English assessment, a progress file should be kept within the department which records the date and comments on Natasha's exposure in school to reading and writing in different genres. If the class teacher had access to such a file at the start of the session s/he would have seen that Natasha had neither read nor written any poetry in her previous time at the school and, knowing that a unit of work on poetry was planned for later in the year, the teacher could have provided targeted support for Natasha along the lines suggested below.
- The teacher should discuss with Natasha and possibly her parents, her knowl-edge of poetry in Russian. She should be encouraged to bring examples of Russian poetry into school, highlighting where the poet creates pictures through the choice of words and trying to translate these word pictures into English or drawing a representation of the images presented. (It is worth noting in this particular case that Edwin Morgan has translated a number of Russian poems into English – *Sovpoems* published by Migrant Press – some of which are also available in Morgan 1996.)
- English teachers should make a collection of images from, for example, Sunday newspaper colour supplements, which can be used to illustrate similes, personification and metaphors, e.g. the sun was a ball of fire; as dusty as the desert; the waves were galloping horses crashing onto the sand; the moon slides slowly across the field. These can be used initially for pupils such as Natasha to match pictures with given phrases and then to create her own similes and metaphors using the pictures as a stimulus.
- Writing of poetry should only be required after considerable exposure to listening to the rhythm of poetry and reading poetry. Natasha could be asked

to write poetry in Russian in the style of a known Russian poet. She could then be given staged targets for writing poetry in English, rather than being set the daunting task of writing a complete poem in the style of a particular poet. For example, after reading and discussing the imagery in *Hawk Roosting*, Natasha could be asked to write two lines (not sentences) about a pigeon (a bird that is frequently found in the school playground) in the style of Ted Hughes, i.e. as if spoken by the pigeon.

These last two possible solutions would also be appropriate for a monolingual English-speaking pupil with little experience of poetry. It will often be the case that by focusing more closely on the language demands of a particular lesson in order to support the bilingual child, the teacher will find ways to increase the learning for all children in the class.

LEE, AGE 13

Lee came from China this year to attend school in the UK for the specific purpose of learning English and enhancing his educational opportunities. He has been placed in Year 8 (1st year) at secondary school. There are four other Chinese pupils in the year who have come to the UK for similar purposes. They are living with two Chinese families in the local community and maintain regular phone and letter contact with their families in China. On their arrival in the school, the pupils immediately enter full-time mainstream education. They are withdrawn from classes twice a week for intensive English tuition and also attend English classes on Saturdays. There is no specific EAL support in any of their classes and none of the subject teachers have had any previous experience of teaching bilingual pupils. Having been at school for six years in China, the pupils are all literate in their first language, which they continue to use on a daily basis to talk to each other and to the families with whom they are boarded. They also use their first language to communicate orally and in writing with their friends and family at home. Lee and his friends are all hard-working, desperate to succeed in British education and to live up to their parents' high expectations.

The class context

In the computing (ICT) class the pupils are learning how to create databases. They are working on producing a database of the addresses and dates of birth of their friends and family, using appropriate field names such as name, house number, street, town, date of birth. The class teacher has assumed that as computing has become a universal language – and she has been told that the Chinese pupils have all studied computing at home – the subject will not present any particular difficulties for them. She has noticed, however, that they tend to sit in a small group at the back of the class and do not produce much work by the end of the day. When asked why they have not contributed the pupils do not respond.

Issues

Although the Chinese pupils are familiar with computers and with databases, the task as presented is laden with cultural and linguistic difficulties for Lee and his friends. The children do not have any friends or family in the town, and are only able to complete a very limited database with the address of the family with whom they are boarding. They are unable to complete a database with the sample field names for their friends and family in China as addresses are constructed in a different format. Although Lee and the other Chinese pupils have sufficient English language to complete many school tasks across the curriculum, they are not able to translate written Chinese into written English, a skill which would be necessary for them to complete this task adequately. A further issue relates to the pupils' difficulties in explaining the problem to the teacher.

Educational challenges

The teacher wishes to enable the Chinese pupils to participate in the mainstream activities of the class. The main challenges for the teacher are:

- how to enable participation without assuming learning difficulties and lowering expectations of the Chinese pupils;
- how to understand the potential difficulties of common computing tasks;
- how to utilise Lee's existing computing skills.

Possible solutions

As for Natasha, there are long-term solutions to be adopted by the school to aid bilingual pupils in addition to specific short-term solutions to be implemented by the class teacher.

- If the school is to continue to recruit and receive Chinese pupils it needs to invest in the recruitment of EAL and bilingual support staff. The computing department should investigate the possibility of purchasing Chinese keyboards or overlays (see Useful Addresses and Websites at the end of this book).
- The school should investigate in-service education and training (INSET) for the whole staff on issues relating to Chinese language, literacy education and assessment. This will help all subject teachers to give more consideration to potential difficulties the children may face in a monolingual English education.

- A member of staff should be appointed with specific responsibility for the welfare of the Chinese pupils and liaison with the families with whom they are boarded.
- In order for the pupils to be able to complete the database as presented, they could be given the initial task of finding out the addresses and birthdays of the other pupils in the class. This would also serve the purposes of initiating more contact between the Chinese pupils and their peers, and of giving the Chinese pupils a contextualised purpose to use a wide range of English language questions, e.g. What is your address? How do you spell that? When were you born? The Chinese pupils could then work in pairs to understand and organise these new forms of information.
- As Lee and the other Chinese pupils are already familiar with the concept of databases, they could be given existing databases to interpret which will help them to become more familiar with the English vocabulary commonly used in field names. In both this solution and the previous one, Lee and his friends should be positively encouraged to use their first language with each other to develop their understanding.
- Although the Chinese pupils have been learning English for three years at home, this has been a very formal English which has not necessarily equipped them for daily routines in the classroom. The teacher should consider the questions pupils need to ask and, with the assistance of a bilingual support teacher or the Chinese families, prepare dual language prompt cards for the newly arrived pupils. These might include questions or phrases such as 'I don't understand', 'Can you help me please?', 'I don't know the English for this'.

From all of these suggestions it can be seen that the ICT teacher – and indeed all subject teachers – has a responsibility not only to teach his/her subject to the bilingual pupils, but also to support their English language learning. This was implied in the Bullock Report (DES 1975: 291): 'all subject teachers need to be more aware of the linguistic demands their specializations make on pupils'. This is not a responsibility to be overly worried about for this heightened awareness can only serve to improve teaching, pupil learning and, as a result, job satisfaction.

It is essential, however, that the classroom teacher should acknowledge that teaching bilingual children does present challenges, and that there is no one answer or magic resource pack that will allay all the teacher's concerns. It can be useful to note down concerns prior to or at the outset of starting to teach a bilingual child, but also to record aspects of your teaching of which you are particularly proud. You should then try to match your skills to your worries as for the teachers in the six case studies presented in this chapter. You need also to be aware that every bilingual child is different, with different language, literacy, educational and cultural backgrounds. Identify what you need to know and how you may begin to find the answers. The two important points to remember are that you have many teaching skills to bring to this new situation and that you are not alone.

The photocopiable proforma on the following page presents a way of recording your concerns, skills, queries and sources of information. Some possible responses are provided for each of these areas but, as indicated, the responses you have will be individual to you, your school context and the children you are teaching.

Once you have begun to identify your concerns, queries, strengths and sources of information you should analyse how your own strengths will help you in the initial period of teaching the bilingual child. For example:

- You have identified that you are good at encouraging quiet children. Analyse how you do this by, for example, enabling the quiet child to work as a partner with a supportive peer. This strategy will also help the bilingual child. By working alongside a supportive child in the class the bilingual child will hear the new language without being pressurised to speak.
- You have identified that you can create stimulating learning environments. This may often involve the use of concrete artifacts to explain complex learning. Again, this is a useful strategy for bilingual children, whereby concrete and pictorial material can be used to assist in the acquisition of new vocabulary.

The next step is to set achievable targets for your teaching of the bilingual child which are drawn from your strengths. Using the examples above, targets for your lessons might be to answer these questions and implement the resultant action:

- In what way can I make the learning in this lesson achievable by a pair of children rather than individuals only?
- What difficult or abstract vocabulary is involved in this lesson and what concrete material and/or pictures would help the bilingual child to acquire this vocabulary?

Concerns, skills, queries and sources

What are my worries?

- How do I teach a child who does not speak English?
- How will I know s/he understands me?
- Do I correct all their mistakes?
- I do not want them to feel different.
- How will I speak to his/her parents?
-
-
-
-
-
-
-
-
-

What are my teaching skills?

- Encouraging quiet children
- Talking to parents
- Creating stimulating learning environments
- Getting to know all the children as individuals
- Differentiating for individual needs
-
-
-
-
-
-
-
-

What do I need to know?

- What language(s) does s/he speak at home?
- Is s/he literate in other languages?
- What are the home literacy practices?
- What is his/her educational history?
- What was his/her previous educational culture?
- What are his/her preferred learning styles?
- What are his/her interests?
-
-
-
-
-
-
-
-

How will I find the answer?

- Ask the child
- Ask the parents
- Ask older siblings
- Ask EAL/bilingual/refugee support teachers
- Research into comparative education practices
-
-
-
-
-
-
-
-

CHAPTER 3

Monolingual Teachers Working with Bilingual Parents

The importance of home–school liaison and partnership with parents has become increasingly recognised in the UK. When considering liaison with the parents of bilingual children, it is vital that schools are aware of the provisions of the Race Relations (Amendment) Act, 2001, which make it unlawful for schools to discriminate in carrying out any of their legal functions, including home–school liaison. The active involvement of parents from bilingual communities is particularly significant in assisting their children's academic achievement (Cummins 1986; Lucas *et al.* 1990; Siraj-Blatchford 1994; Gregory 1997; Department for Education and Employment (DfEE) 1998). All children, teachers and parents want and deserve the best education that can be provided. For education to be the most effective possible, these three groups need to be able to communicate. Where a gap exists between the language/culture of the school and the home it can cause frustration and anxiety for all participants, but this need not be the case.

This chapter will consider ways of fostering effective home–school liaison in situations where the parents and teachers do not share a common language. Communication with parents, homework and dealing with extended leave will be the major liaison issues examined through case studies derived from actual practice.

The DfEE produced guidelines (2000) on raising achievement levels for minority ethnic pupils. These guidelines – which include a summary of good practice in schools where effective parental involvement has been achieved – will be referred to throughout this chapter as an indicator of how suggestions in the chapter match with effective practice already in place.

Parents' meetings

Home support for education is viewed as an aid to success and parents in most schools are encouraged to attend biannual or annual parents' meetings to discuss their children's academic progress. A common concern among teachers regarding the involvement of bilingual parents in their children's education centres on the difficulties of communicating due to teachers and parents not sharing a language. Radiating from this central concern are connected concerns that education is not viewed in the same way by parents who do not speak English, and that parents can do little to help their children because the curriculum is delivered in English.

Blackledge (2000) interviewed a number of bilingual parents (in this case Bengali mothers) and found several common issues regarding home–school liaison which can be applied in other bilingual situations:

- The parents may not have a command of the language of the school.
- The school may not provide appropriate interpreters for the parents.
- The parents may work in the evenings.
- Children may be used as interpreters.
- The parents are not empowered to ask questions of the teacher.

Parents who do not share the language of the school miss opportunities to find out about their child's education, not due to lack of interest but due to the structures of the school not facilitating the parents' attendance at parents' evenings.

MARK, AGE 5

Mark is a five-year-old Cantonese-speaking boy. His parents both work in a local Chinese restaurant. They did not attend the first parents' evening for the parents of new children and have not responded to a letter, written in English, sent home with Mark, asking them to contact the school if they wish to discuss Mark's progress. The class teacher would like to meet Mark's parents, particularly as she has some concerns about what Mark understands in class, but she does not know what to do.

The school promotes parental involvement and explains the purpose of parents' nights in its handbook, although this document is not provided in any language other than English.

Issues

The parents did not attend the official opportunity to meet the teacher. This is possibly due to them not being available for meetings in the evening. It may also be due to them believing – as did a number of the parents in Blackledge's study – that they would not understand what was being said. There is also the fact that they may not understand the purpose of the meeting. They have not responded to a letter sent home. This letter may not have arrived. The parents may not be literate in English. The letter offered contact *if* the parents wanted to discuss Mark's progress; the parents may not see this as an invitation to discuss Mark's education with his teacher.

Possible solutions

Rather than a letter, a phone call could be made to the parents, inviting them to come to the school. This personal contact could discuss a time when it would be suitable for the parents to visit the teacher, rather than leaving the onus on the parents to make the arrangements. A phone call would also help to establish if there might be a need for an interpreter. The school needs to enable the teacher to meet with the parents during the school day, perhaps by providing class cover for half an hour. An open-door policy would enable the parents to come to the school at a convenient time rather than the fixed and formal nature of the appointment system. The school will also need to provide an interpreter if necessary (through the education authority in the first instance). In the longer term the school will require, with authority assistance, to translate the school handbook into the home languages of its pupils. These suggestions tally with comments made in parental interviews (with black parents at a primary school) quoted in the DfEE guidelines to demonstrate best practice in school liaison: "'I can come in, I don't need to make an appointment, and have a quick chat with my son's teacher at any time." "If anything happens they'll phone me up and I'll pop in and check on him to see how he's getting on, and things like that." "We always get letters home, always, about what they're doing – newsletters always come home."' (DfEE 2000: 23).

RIZWANA, AGE 9 AND NAHEEDA, AGE 6
Rizwana is a nine-year-old Punjabi-speaking girl. Her teacher, Gwen, is very concerned at the lack of contact with Rizwana's parents:

Gwen: *Our point of communication is Dad. Mum as far as we know doesn't speak any English or very much at all so she doesn't come near the school, and nice as Mr Kaur* [Rizwana's father] *is, I don't think his English is all that great and it's not easy. I don't always feel we hit the mark.*

Mary teaches Naheeda, Rizwana's six-year-old sister, and has raised similar concerns:

Mary: *When I was trying to specify Naheeda's problems* [to Mr Kaur] *and be specific about it, I don't think he fully understood . . . all that I was trying to get across . . . Mrs Smith* [the EAL teacher] *has spent quite a lot of time with him too, trying to give him guidance to let him know how he could help Naheeda, but that again I don't think was carried through.*

Issues

Mary and Gwen have assumed that the girls' father's English has not been adequate to understand the difficulties they were experiencing at school. This may well be the case, but it has left the teachers with the belief that the parents' limitations in English are causing the child difficulties. Gwen has identified that that there is a problem for the mother liaising with the school as it operates in a language she does not share.

Possible solutions

Some of the issues raised in relation to Mark's parents can be applied here. There is also a need for school staff to adopt the parents' perspective when considering home–school liaison. A change in perspective would see Gwen saying: 'We don't speak any Punjabi at all so we're not really able to discuss with Rizwana's mum.' Adopting this stance would then highlight the need for interpreters and remove the blame from the parents. In addition, it is important for the school to actively encourage minority language parents into the school by establishing a multilingual, multicultural ethos. As suggested in the DfEE guidelines (2000: 23), if schools hold family events such as assemblies to encourage parents to stay on after they have brought their children to school in the morning, this would help the parents to get to know the school and the teachers. Ideas for developing a multilingual, multicultural ethos will be further discussed in Chapter 4.

It is clearly frustrating for Gwen, Mary and Mrs Smith who have not been enabled in their pre-service or in-service training to communicate with parents who do not share the dominant language. There is a need for a school and authority INSET to further address the issues of working with bilingual parents that are identified in this chapter.

In this instance several teachers in the school are experiencing similar frustrations trying to communicate with bilingual parents. Rather than leave this frustration to develop into more serious concerns, head teachers could allocate responsibility to a specific teacher for the development of more effective liaison with bilingual parents in some of the ways suggested in this chapter. This teacher – or another, named member of staff – could be allocated responsibility as a direct telephone line link for bilingual families, ensuring that when parents phone the school they can speak to someone they know and trust (DfEE 2000: 21). This teacher could also teach the rest of the staff how to greet the parents in their home language when they come to the school, thus helping to establish a welcoming ethos.

BILLY, AGE 9 AND JO, AGE 7

North Primary is in a seaside town and has very few bilingual children. In the past the parents of the bilingual children have been fluent in English and at ease in the school context. A Chinese family has recently arrived in the town. Billy and Jo have enrolled in Primary 4 and Primary 2. The school has biannual parents' evenings which are generally well attended. Billy and Jo's parents attended the most recent evening meeting and brought Billy with them. Megan, Billy's class teacher, told me:

Billy's Mum and Dad's English is broken so Billy translated what I was saying for them but I don't know what he said to them and I couldn't say very much because it was about Billy. And they didn't say anything to me; they just smiled and nodded.

(Note: Primary 2 is the second year of primary education in Scotland and Primary 4 the fourth year.)

Issues

In many cases, bilingual parents do not expect an interpreter to be present at the parents' evening and therefore bring the child or an older sibling to interpret for them if the teacher does not share their language. This causes more discomfort for the teacher than the parents as this is not a usual way of communicating in UK schools. In this case, the communication was not two-way, possibly due in part to Megan's discomfort with discussing the child's progress in front of him.

Possible solutions

In addition to the solutions suggested in the earlier case studies, there seems to be a need for clear written explanations in community languages about the purpose and process of parents' evenings in order that all parties concerned can gain maximum benefit.

As the demography of the UK changes (as outlined in Chapter 1), schools need to recognise that not only will many parents not share the language of the school, but also they will have very different experiences of schools and education. Where cultural norms differ this can result in communication difficulties being exacerbated. Seeking the answers to the questions posed in the forms in Chapter 1 will help teachers to address some of these communication difficulties.

Literacy homework

In Chapter 1 the dilemma faced by Elsie when she realised that the school and Chih Hai's parents did not share the same approach to reading was presented. What can be done in this situation?

- Elsie's initial response was to stop sending the book home with Chih Hai. As was pointed out in Chapter 1, the effect of this was to deny Chih Hai's parents the opportunity to support their son's education. Furthermore, it sends signals to Chih Hai that there are things he cannot do and educational practices he cannot engage in because he is not monolingual in English.
- The next solution Elsie considered was to ask other Chinese adults to help with Chih Hai's reading. While this would enable Chih Hai to do the same homework as his monolingual peers it would not involve his parents in his education.
- Many readers may question the practice that is under discussion and argue that more effective homework should be set for all the children in the class. However, the reality for many class teachers is that they do not have the autonomy to deviate from school practices and must operate within the school norms.

Any solutions to this dilemma therefore require a number of factors to be in place:

1. Chih Hai should have the same opportunity as his monolingual peers to share his school work with his parents.
2. Chih Hai's parents must be enabled to assist their son with the acquisition of school literacy.
3. Chih Hai must be enabled to make links between home and school literacy practices and the languages of home and school.

The school should extend an invitation to Chih Hai's parents – and any other bilingual parents – to visit the classroom and the teacher to see the resources that are used for learning and how they are employed. An interpreter, who may be a family member, a friend or a member of the community, should also be invited to this meeting. These suggestions again conform with DfEE guidelines (2000: 23), which propose that schools should provide comprehensive information on curriculum issues and homework, and run classes for parents. In presenting the reading scheme to Chih Hai's parents, Elsie should focus on the importance of Chih Hai understanding the meaning of the text. She should encourage his parents to talk to him about the pictures from the marked pages in the language they normally use for communicating in the home. It is the school's role, not the parents', to help Chih Hai with decoding the print.

It is important that Chih Hai's parents recognise the value of continuing to

Jim and his dad went
to Gran's house with the presents.
They got on the bus.

The bus went along the street
and it went past a school.
It went past a paper shop.
It went past big shops
and it stopped in Park Street.

Figure 3.1 Extract from reading scheme (Link-Up)

communicate with him in the home language and they should be helped to understand that continued development of his first language will increase his ability to acquire English (Cummins and Swain 1986). It was suggested in Chapter 1 that teachers should collect written samples of the languages which the child uses at home and display these in the classroom. Chih Hai's parents should be asked for some written Cantonese samples. This will reinforce to Chih Hai and his family that the home language is valued and will also remind the teacher of the difference in the written language of the classroom and that which Chih Hai sees at home. Figure 3.1 shows an extract from the reading scheme in use in Chih Hai's classroom. The pictures contain much environmental print. Consider how to model the questions Chih Hai's parents could ask him about the pictures.

In this extract from the Link-Up reading scheme (Holmes McDougall 1986), there is a considerable potential for discussion about the picture that will aid Chih Hai's understanding of the text. Table 3.1 offers some suggestions and identifies how a range of purposes can be met by different questions. It is thus important for the teacher to model questions and discussion points to avoid an over-emphasis on literal, closed questions.

The suggestions offered can be applied to literacy homework for a range of ages and stages at primary school. They accord with proposals within the National Literacy Strategy in England and Wales. It is important that the teacher acknowl-

Table 3.1 Modelling questions for literacy homework

Sample questions and discussion points	Purpose
• Where do we go when we get the bus?	• This contextualises the story content for Chih Hai and his parents and enables Chih Hai to relate the story to his own experience.
• How do we get the bus to stop?	• This cultural knowledge will help Chih Hai to contribute to class discussions about the story content.
• Where will Jim and his dad go on the bus?	• This helps Chih Hai to understand the text surrounding the picture and to predict what might happen in the story.
• I wonder how many stops that might be.	• This will encourage Chih Hai to speculate.
• Why are there no leaves on the trees?	• This will enable close examination of the illustration and engagement with meaning.

edges the difference between the role of the school and the role of the home in supporting literacy development. Furthermore, the teacher needs to give consideration not only to developing the child's ability to decode the text and to understand what has been read but also to extending the purposes for which the child can use the English language. In the example offered above, the modelled questions go beyond the text to help the child reflect, predict and speculate. This is in line with the Reading to Reflect on the Writer's Ideas and Craft strand of the 5–14 National Guidelines for English Language in Scotland (Scottish Office Education Department (SOED) 1991) and with the National Literacy Strategy in England and Wales, enabling Chih Hai to actively engage in discussion of the text.

Further discussion about the identification of purposes, or functions, of language in planning the curriculum for bilingual children can be found in Chapter 5. The photocopiable format at the end of the chapter should help teachers to plan parental support for homework for bilingual pupils. It should be kept in a pupil file and passed each year to the class teacher(s). It should be updated annually particularly with regard to the focus for questioning.

Extended leave

Many bilingual pupils accompany their families on extended visits to the family's country of origin for which they may have extended leave from school. Such extended heritage visits during the school year can be a source of concern to teachers, as in the case of Mark's teacher. Mark went to Hong Kong with his family for six weeks during his first year at primary school in Scotland. His teacher expressed concerns that when he came back he had forgotten everything he had learned before he went away. Such a situation, whereby a child and his or her family is blamed for the child's learning needs, can result in a lowering of self-esteem (Archibald 1994). Focusing on the gap in the child's formal learning rather than the bilingual and bicultural skills which the child brings to the classroom effectively discriminates against the child and family. Cummins (1996: 178) has stressed the educational benefits that accrue to the whole school community when the linguistic and cultural resources of its bilingual population are recognised and valued.

Some teachers have expressed concerns about providing homework for children who go on extended heritage visits on the grounds that the children could not do the homework without the teacher input or that the books may be mislaid during the journey. It is important – particularly in the light of the Race Relations (Amendment) Act of 2001 – that schools have a policy to support children who go on extended heritage visits. The act makes it 'unlawful for an educational establishment to discriminate by refusing to or omitting to afford its pupils or students access to its benefits, facilities or services'. One way of ensuring this does not occur when pupils go on extended heritage visits might be by the provision of study booklets such as those produced by the City of Coventry Minority Group Support Service or by Falkirk Council Bilingual and Traveller Pupil Support Service (BATPUSS). The content of such booklets could involve investigations using home language skills and collation of the information using English language literacy skills. The tasks can also provide information about the heritage culture which will be of use to schools in the UK. They can also provide opportunities for the pupils to reflect on their bilingualism and biculturalism. Sample material from the Falkirk secondary booklet is reproduced in Figure 3.2.

The DfEE report (2000: 23) highlights the fact that those schools which had been effective in actively involving ethnic minority parents had given particular attention to such issues as extended leave to visit relatives overseas.

This chapter has stressed the vital importance of effective home–school links, yet it is an area of considerable concern for teachers as has been demonstrated in the case studies. Accepting the need to develop personal and school practice in relation to bilingual parents is an important first step in improving home–school liaison.

Suggestions for initial targets for the school:

- In preparation for writing an information leaflet for bilingual parents, discuss the purposes of parental liaison and homework.
- Identify a liaison member of staff for bilingual families and specify their duties.
- Identify the source of translating and interpretation services in the education authority.
- Plan a series of parental workshops across the curriculum.
- Develop materials to issue to bilingual pupils going on extended heritage visits.

Planning parental support for literacy homework

Session _____ Class _____ Teacher _____

Texts to be used this year in class

_____

_____

_____

_____

_____

Date of parents' workshop _____

Name of child _____

Language spoken at home _____

Name and contact details of translator _____

_____

Who attended the workshop? _____

What purposes were emphasised in questioning and discussion?

_____

_____

HERITAGE VISIT TO PAKISTAN

ARCHITECTURE

Important Buildings

You will see many wonderful buildings on your visit (i.e. a mosque, a temple, a college or a palace perhaps). Use pencils or paint to draw any buildings which you see. You can also bring back any photographs or postcards which show such buildings.

Religious Buildings

You may visit a place of interest, like the Shish Mahal or Jahangir's Mosque. Write a report about it describing the purpose of the place and where it is located. You should also include details such as the interior and exterior design of the building and the decorations.

Find out about the Mughal Empire. What buildings, forts and gardens can still be seen today? Research into Jahangir, his son Shah Jahan and his son Aurangzeb.

Modern Buildings

Are there any modern buildings which have really impressed you? Perhaps it was an airport! What features impressed you? You should also describe the building materials and any features of its design. If possible, provide a picture of this building.

Look at some homes in the town or village where you stay. Do you notice any structural differences (i.e. building materials, layout etc)? Describe these differences.

فنِ تعمیر۔

اہم عمارات

کسی مسجد ، مندر ، کالج یا کسی محل کی صورت میں آپ حیرت انگیز عمارتیں دیکھیں گے ۔ اپنی پنسل یا برش سے بنائے ہوئے ان کے خاکے ، تصویریں یا پوسٹ کارڈ اپنے ساتھ لائیں ۔

مذہبی عمارات

اگر آپ شاہی قلعہ یا شاہی مسجد یا جہانگیر کا مقبرہ دیکھیں تو یہ بتائیں کہ یہ عمارتیں کیوں بنیں اور یہ کہاں واقع ہیں ؟ ان کے بیرونی اور اندرونی ڈیزائن اور آرائش کا حال بیان کریں ۔

مغل سلطنت کے بارے معلومات حاصل کریں ۔ آج بھی کون کون سی عمارتیں ، قلعے اور باغات دیکھے جا سکتے ہیں ؟ جہانگیر ، شاہ جہاں اور اورنگ زیب کے بارے میں ریسرچ کریں ۔

جدید عمارات

اگر جدید عمارتوں میں سے کسی نے آپ کو متاثر کیا تو اس کی کس چیز سے آپ متاثر ہوئے ۔ اس میں استعمال ہونے والے عمارتی سامان اور اس کے ڈیزائن کا ذکر کریں اور اسکی تصویر ساتھ لیتے آئیں ۔

جس شہر یا دیہات میں آپ ٹھہرے ہوں اس کے گھروں پر نگاہ ڈالیں اگر آپ کو ان کی تعمیر میں کوئی فرق نظر آتے ہوں تو بیان کریں ۔

Figure 3.2   Extracts from Falkirk County Council BATPUSS booklet for secondary pupils: 'Heritage Visit to Pakistan'

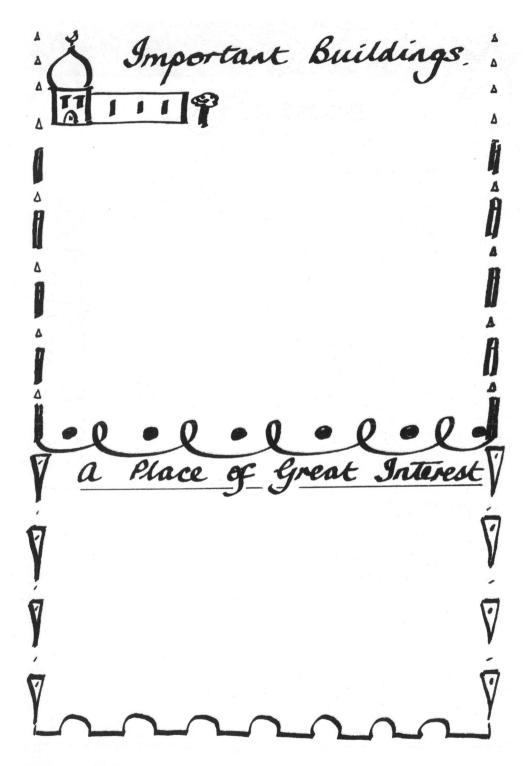

Figure 3.2 Continued

HERITAGE VISIT TO PAKISTAN

ART AND DESIGN

Carpets

Look at carpets being made. Take photographs of the finished products and the people making them. What techniques are used in the manufacturing of carpets? Describe the materials which are used in the manufacturing process (i.e. textures, colour tones and patterns). If possible, you could even make up your own designs for carpets.

Crafts

Watch people making jewellery or weaving fabrics. Try to find out the products which the craftsmen/women use. You could even bring back a small sample of such material. This would enable you to make these samples into a collage. Again, if possible, try and get a photograph of these crafts.

Would it be possible for you to make something whilst you are staying in Pakistan? If you have access to clay or other materials, you could make things like pots. If you are unable to bring back what you make, then you could always take a photograph of the finished product for proof.

Look at mosaics and tiles. Study the patterns and designs. Copy some of these patterns or make your own.

Calligraphy is the art of handwriting and is at the heart of Islamic Art. Look for examples on panels in a mosque. Copy some examples or bring back pictures of some.

آرٹ اور ڈیزائن

قالین

قالین بافی کو بغور دیکھیں ۔ تیار شدہ قالینوں اور انہیں بنانے والوں کی تصاویر لیں ۔ قالین بافی میں کون سا خام مال استعمال ہوتا ہے ؟

دستکاریاں

لوگوں کو زیور بناتے اور پارچہ بافی کرتے دیکھیں ۔ یہ معلوم کریں کہ دستکار کون کون سی چیزیں استعمال کرتے ہیں ۔ ان کے نمونے ساتھ لائیں اور ان دست کاریوں کی تصاویر لیں ۔ اگر آپ مٹی یا دوسری چیزیں حاصل کر سکیں تو برتن نما چیزیں خود بھی بنائیں اور ان کی تصاویر بطور ثبوت ساتھ لائیں

ٹائلیں ، ریزہ کاری اور جڑاوہ کام ہوتا دیکھیں اور کچھ نمونوں اور ڈیزائنوں کی نقل اتاریں یا خود اپنے نمونے تیار کریں

اسلامی آرٹ میں خطاطی کو بنیادی حیثیت حاصل ہے ۔ مساجد میں اور کتبوں پر اس کی مثالیں ملاحظہ کریں ۔ ان کی نقل اتاریں اور کچھ نمونے ساتھ لائیں

Figure 3.2 Continued

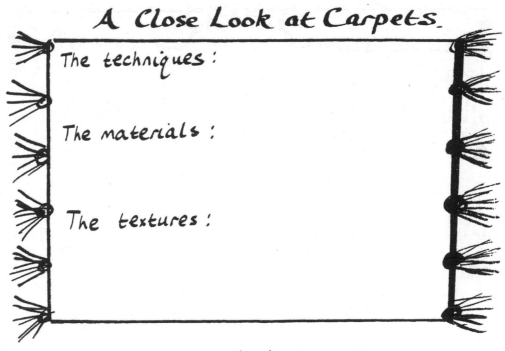

The colours and tones :

The patterns:

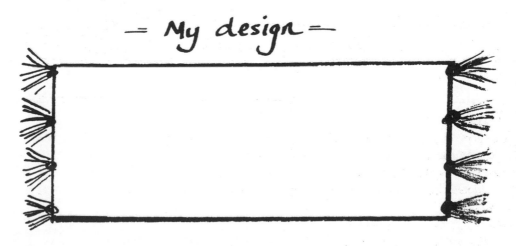

Figure 3.2 Continued

CHAPTER 4

Valuing the Multilingual and Multicultural Nature of the School Population

Since the numbers of children in UK schools from non-white, non-European cultures began to increase in the 1960s, much has been written about the need to make the school and the curriculum more multicultural in order to respond to the needs of children from cultures beyond the indigenous British culture. This view of culture is flawed as it sees cultures as discrete and static entities rather than combined and dynamic. Within this view, approaches to this multiculturalisation have been varied in focus and intent. (The history of multicultural education has been discussed elsewhere; see Dhondy 1981; Brandt 1986; Smyth 2001b.) A major criticism of multicultural education has been that it has tended to take a 'three S's approach' (Troyna and Williams 1986). Troyna and Williams argued against a response to multiculturalisation that attempted to focus on the exotic components of cultures such as saris, samosas and steel bands, i.e. the three S's. They argued that this interpretation of pluralism was not only tokenistic, but served to contain and defuse the three R's: resistance, rejection and rebellion. Within their argument, multicultural education is one of the causes of underachievement among minority ethnic pupils. This argument is beyond the scope of this book and can be pursued in the suggested references and elsewhere.

This chapter will use case studies to show how schools can develop a more inclusive and non-tokenistic approach to all children's languages and cultures.

DARJIT, AGE 11

Darjit is 11 years old. He came to the UK from Bangladesh when he was eight years old and has been at school in Scotland for three years. Jackie, the class teacher, reports that Darjit is a pleasant child to teach as he is responsive to learning.

Jackie does not know a great deal about Darjit's background before he came to Scotland:

His personal project is on Sikhism and that's the only reference that's made there to any non-Scottish way of life. Darjit doesn't remember much about

> *Bangladesh. He knows that's where he's come from and he can show you it on the map and stuff but not be willing to tell you anything else and I think there might be a reason for this . . . You could be treading on some sort of religious icons for all you know but I don't ask. As far as I'm concerned he's Scottish although as far as he's concerned it's Bangladesh whenever I ask him.*

Issues

This discussion with Jackie highlights a number of issues around multicultural education for mainstream teachers. Implicitly, Jackie equates religion with ethnic background – Sikhism is described as 'non-Scottish'. This belief is reinforced by the 5–14 Guidelines for Religious and Moral Education which start from the premise that religious education should be based on Christianity, with tolerance of 'other world religions'. While this belief is enshrined in the curriculum it will be difficult for teachers to have a starting point which recognises all religions in Scotland as Scottish, or in the UK as British.

Jackie reports that Darjit 'doesn't remember much about Bangladesh'. However, it is not clear whether Jackie has given him the opportunity to 'remember about Bangladesh'. She is reluctant to ask him about his previous experience in case she 'could be treading on some sort of religious icons'. This fear of getting things wrong is further discussed in Chapter 7 and is symptomatic of a teacher education system, prevalent throughout the UK, which does not adequately prepare teachers for responding to the needs of pupils from linguistic, cultural or class backgrounds outwith a white, middle-class monolingual 'norm'. Teachers need support to learn how to talk to their pupils from a cultural background different to their own.

A third significant issue arising from this short discussion with Jackie is that she seems to believe that it is in Darjit's best interests to deny his cultural background: 'As far as I'm concerned he's Scottish although as far as he's concerned it's Bangladesh whenever I ask him.' This appears to be an expression on Jackie's part that children should be integrated into the mainstream. While integration is indeed desirable it should not be an integration which rejects cultural heritage, but rather an integration in which diversity of cultural heritage is an enriching factor. This issue is also further discussed in Chapter 7 which considers the roots of the cultural models held by teachers about bilingualism and multiculturalism.

Darjit is in the final year of his primary education and along with the rest of the class has been encouraged to engage in a personal project of his own choosing. The purpose of this exercise is to develop the children's research and presentation skills. A number of children in Darjit's class have chosen to do their projects about contemporary celebrities from sport or entertainment. Darjit has chosen to do his project on Sikhism, thereby clearly demonstrating that he is not, as Jackie suspects, unwilling or unable to discuss his background.

DARJIT (continued)

During my research I had the opportunity to see Darjit working on his personal project and he talked to me enthusiastically and knowledgeably about his research. Pointing to a world map he had drawn Darjit told me that his ancestors ('my grandfather's grandfathers') came to the Punjab from Russia, through China and Nepal, then became Sikhs. He then told me about the Indian Wars of Partition (1947).

I asked Darjit if he spoke Punjabi, to which he replied 'haa' (Punjabi: yes). He then told me he does not read or write Punjabi, but he does read 'The Holy Book' in Punjabi (The Guru Granth Sahib).

Many teachers recognise that their bilingual pupils have skills and knowledge that they are unable to use in school due to the limiting nature of the curriculum. Darjit very clearly displayed pride in his linguistic, cultural and religious heritage. He was eager to share his knowledge which had come to him from his family and religious community rather than from school. I shall now demonstrate how the school can be enabled to value and utilise Darjit's knowledge and pride in order to help create a more inclusive school. Only a small amount of information is presented about Darjit in the above case study, but already it enables us to answer certain questions, as presented below, about Darjit's knowledge and skills that go beyond the boundaries of formal curriculum knowledge.

This model of questioning can be used as a template for teachers to consider the knowledge and skills that all their pupils bring to school.

What does Darjit know?

Darjit knows about the historical origins of his religion. He has an understanding of issues related to forced migration and religious wars. He recognises the relationship of geographical locations and has knowledge of historical events. From his reading in Punjabi of the Guru Granth Sahib, he knows that not all scripts are written in the same way.

What might Darjit know?

Darjit may know about Sikh religious practices and places of worship. However, this cannot be assumed as Darjit lives in an area of Scotland where there are few Sikhs and no Sikh temple (Gurdwara). Given that he was eight years old at the time of his arrival in the UK, Darjit may know about immigration procedures and legislation.

What can Darjit do?

Darjit can communicate orally in at least one language other than English, i.e. Punjabi. He can also read aloud in Punjabi from a set text.

How does this link to the National Curriculum/5-14 Guidelines?

The knowledge and skills which Darjit has are very clearly linked to the school curriculum; the table below indicates some of the ways in which these relate to both the National Curriculum for England and Wales and the 5–14 Curriculum Guidelines for Scotland. Using similar questions to those applied to Darjit and the other case studies in this chapter, and adding their knowledge of their own class and the curricular guidelines which apply to their teaching, teachers will be able to identify ways in which the bilingual pupils in their class are achieving across the curriculum. It is these specific skills and this specific knowledge of the individual pupils which should then be used to enhance the multilingual and multicultural nature of the classroom and school, rather than the tokenistic '3S's' approach outlined at the beginning of the chapter.

Curriculum and Assessment in Scotland National Guidelines 5–14

English Language: Knowledge About Language, Talking and Listening – audience awareness, Reading for Information, Functional Writing

Religious and Moral Education: (NB this is a statutory curricular area in Scotland.) Other World Religions: Sacred Writings, Stories and Key Figures; Personal Search: Moral Values and Attitudes, Ultimate Questions

Environmental Studies: People and Place, People in the Past, People in Society

National Curriculum for England and Wales

English: KS2 Speaking and Listening skills, Reading for Information, Range of Purposes for Writing

Geography: KS2 Knowledge and Understanding of Places and of Patterns and Processes

---

How can I find out what pupils know and can do beyond the constraints of the curriculum?

The personal project has been an excellent route for finding out about Darjit's knowledge and skills but it was accidental. Had Darjit chosen, along with many of his peers, to undertake research related to, for example, the Premier Football League, much of his knowledge would have remained hidden. Children should not be put on the spot and asked to tell the class all they know about, for example, Sikhism or the Chinese New Year. If considering this, teachers should imagine their response if asked in a new country and a new language to tell their peers all about, for example, how Saint George's Day or Burns' Night is celebrated in their home country. Even if they are fairly confident individuals, it is likely they would run out of things to say after a couple of sentences. It is important therefore for teachers to enable pupils to display their knowledge by using topics in the classroom, such as 'Where We Came From' or 'Languages We Speak', in which all the pupils participate. Sample outlines for such topics can be found at the end of this chapter.

The next case study presents a much younger child than Darjit, from a different linguistic and cultural background.

MARK, AGE 5

Mark is in his first year of primary school. He did not attend nursery school prior to starting at primary and had very little English when he came to school. His family are from Hong Kong and own a Chinese restaurant in the town. Morag, the class teacher, does not know a great deal about Mark's background and has not met his parents. She tells me that this is because they work in the evenings when parents' meetings are held in the school. She also tells me that Mark goes straight to the restaurant after school and does his reading homework there.

I observed in the class one day a few weeks before Xmas. The class was doing a religious education topic about Xmas, during which the teacher was telling the children the story of the Nativity. The teacher drew a picture of the Nativity on the board, which the children were required to copy. The girl beside Mark had added three stars in the sky to her picture:

☆ ☆ ☆

I noticed Mark looking at the girl's stars and drawing these symbols at the top of his page. As he drew, the symbols began to resemble Chinese characters (see Figure 4.1). As far as the teacher knew Mark was not literate in Cantonese, but it was later confirmed to me by a teacher who is literate in Chinese that the symbols on Mark's paper were in fact childish efforts to write Chinese characters. The act of drawing the representational star had reminded Mark of writing in the script of his parents.

Issues

What does Mark know?

Like Darjit, Mark knows that not all scripts are written in the same way.

What might Mark know?

As Mark's parents work in a restaurant and he is known to spend time there it is possible he knows about table setting and clearing, menus, taking orders, preparing, cooking and serving food.

What can Mark do?

Mark can attempt to write Chinese characters although he has not had any formal instruction in this skill.

Figure 4.1   From stars to Chinese script: Mark, age 5

How does this link to the National Curriculum/5–14 Guidelines?

Curriculum and Assessment in Scotland National Guidelines 5–14

English Language: Knowledge About Language

Environmental Studies: People in Society

National Curriculum

English: Writing KS1: presentation and planning skills

Geography: Enquiry KS1: communicating in different ways

How can I find out what pupils know and can do beyond the constraints of the curriculum?

Finding out about Mark's developing knowledge and skills was coincidental and Morag freely told me she would not have noticed the Cantonese characters in his drawing. In order to enable such young children to discuss and demonstrate their knowledge of other writing systems, teachers should collect and display samples of writing in scripts other than English in the classroom. The writing corner should have examples of, for example, Chinese menus and posters for Hindi films. Dual language books should be displayed and talked about during the Literacy Hour. Inspiring ideas and discussion about the use of languages other than English with young children are to be found in the work of Charmian Kenner (1999).

To enable all children to feel comfortable in the classroom environment, teachers must not assume that all home backgrounds are the same. It may be difficult for Mark to engage with a home corner with small-scale pots and other utensils, for example, when he is used to an industrial-sized kitchen. Teachers should also think about the provision of cooking and eating implements in the home corner such as chopsticks and woks.

Refugee pupils

Since the dispersal procedures introduced by the Immigration and Asylum Act (1999), schools across the UK have had refugee and asylum-seekers' children on their rolls. Within this text, the word refugee will be used to also cover asylum-seekers' children, as *there is educational entitlement for all children, no matter their legal status.* (An asylum seeker is a person who has applied to the Home Office for Refugee status; a refugee is a person who, as a result of their asylum application, has either been awarded Exceptional Leave to remain, which is a discretionary status allowing temporary permission to stay in the UK, or Convention status which permits permanent residence in the UK.) Education authorities have responded in a range of ways to the specific needs of refugee children who, in addition to the language needs identified for all the children in this book, face hostility from much of the mainstream press which adds to the specific trauma of their situation of having fled their country of origin.

Closs *et al.* (1999) conducted a two-year research study into the school experience of refugee children in Scotland, which identified – from the viewpoint of refugee pupils, their parents and school staff – those education responses perceived as constructive, empathetic and practical (Closs *et al.* 1999: 6). The 12 pupils interviewed within the research identified six major issues which affected their educational experience in Scotland (Arshad *et al.* 1999):

1 Coping with a different system
  The pupils interviewed all recognised significant differences between the education system in Scotland and that in their country of origin. This could lead to uncertainty about how to behave and how to relate to teachers.
2 Language issues
  The onus was frequently on the pupils to seek extra help with their English language when they already had some knowledge of English. The majority of pupils wanted extra English tuition and several expressed the concern they were losing their home language.
3 Friendships
  A number of the pupils expressed the belief that a multiracial school was important for helping them to make friends and to feel more comfortable.
4 Name calling, bullying and racism
  All but one of the 12 pupils interviewed had experienced such incidents at school and many felt that nothing had been done about it by the school despite the incidents being reported.
5 Support
  A significant issue here was the expression of the need for more support when choosing subjects for exams.
6 Issues of inclusion
  Particularly significant for this chapter about how schools can develop a more inclusive and non-tokenistic approach to all children's languages and cultures is the fact that the pupils did not welcome attempts to include them by drawing attention to them or their countries as individuals.

MARIELA, AGE 9

Mariela is nine years old and has arrived in an inner-city primary school as part of the dispersal of asylum seekers. For the last term she has received English language support within the school in a base for refugee children and has been integrated into the mainstream classroom for art, music and physical education. Funding for the base has now been withdrawn and Mariela is educated full time in the Year 4 class, where the teacher has no specific knowledge of teaching either refugee children or children for whom English is not their first language. Mariela is a bright, sociable child. She does not yet produce a great deal of written or spoken English but she appears to understand the class teachers' instructions.

Issues

Many of the issues and solutions for Mariela's teacher are similar to those for Sunita's teacher in Chapter 1; she has no experience of working with pupils who have linguistic, cultural and personal needs such as Mariela. As indicated in the discussion above, Mariela, in common with many refugee children, may be subjected to name calling or bullying. In addition to the traumas which Mariela may have had to face due to her position as a refugee, she has now had her form of education changed yet again – from the refugee base to the mainstream classroom – and she will need support for this change.

Possible solutions

Mariela's teacher should find out about Mariela's background (as proposed in Chapter 1) and also consider the targets listed at the end of Chapter 1. Responses to the education of Sunita in Chapter 2 are also appropriate here. In addition, Mariela's teacher should undertake the audit presented at the end of Chapter 2. It is important that, in attempts to include Mariela in the mainstream classroom, her teacher does not inadvertently draw undue attention to Mariela or her country. As indicated in Closs *et al.* 1999 (discussed above), being put on the spot was not welcomed by the refugee pupils. Rather, the teacher should consider, as for Darjit and Mark, what Mariela knows, can do, may know and may be able to do. The teacher should then plan opportunities for Mariela to use and demonstrate her existing knowledge and skills across the curriculum.

It is essential for Mariela that she feels able to approach teaching staff about any concerns she may have and that she knows the school will take these concerns seriously. The DfEE guidelines have highlighted this in the section on culture and ethos

(DfEE 2000: 16–19). The school needs to establish a forum whereby pupils and parents can air their concerns. INSET must address the nature of racism and the implementation and monitoring of a school anti-racist policy. As will be discussed in Chapter 7, it is important that the school's anti-racist policy informs the policy for bilingual learners. It is important that all sections of the school community (parents, pupils and ancillary staff as well as teachers) are included in the development of a policy. This will foster a climate of commitment and ownership which is essential for the success of such a policy. Furthermore, an inclusive working party emphasises a commitment on the part of the school to equity and empowerment.

What does Mariela know?

Mariela is beginning to know about the school curriculum and organisation in the UK. She has experienced the UK immigration procedures at first-hand. She has travelled extensively and used a range of transport.

What might Mariela know?

As she is nine years old, it is likely that Mariela has experienced another form of schooling, although this will have been interrupted.

What can Mariela do?

Mariela can adapt – to different cultures, school organisations and languages.

How does this link to the National Curriculum/5–14 Guidelines?

Curriculum and Assessment in Scotland National Guidelines 5–14

Environmental Studies: People in Society

National Curriculum

Geography: KS2 Knowledge and Understanding of Places and of Patterns and Processes

---

How can I find out what pupils know and can do beyond the constraints of the curriculum?

Mariela should be enabled to demonstrate her knowledge, skills and understandings from her previous education.

- She should be given numeracy tasks which do not require English literacy skills, i.e. where the mathematical content of the task is not hidden by lengthy text, as is often the case in maths textbooks (see Chapter 7).
- The teacher should plan to involve Mariela in collaborative learning tasks (see Chapter 7) to enable her to learn and demonstrate her cognitive ability across the curriculum without the requirement to produce extensive written or oral English.
- The teacher should sensitively plan global citizenship topics such as those in this chapter, which will allow Mariela to make meaningful contributions when she is ready and to recognise that her experiences are valued.

Education for citizenship

Education for citizenship is a current area of educational debate in many countries of the world (Luthar *et al.* 2001). The debate incorporates a wide range of political questions which are beyond the scope of this book, such as *Who is a citizen?* and *For whose benefit is citizenship?* Within this book, I shall use the terminology devised by Oxfam (1997) in suggesting that education should enable pupils to become global citizens who:

- are aware of the wider world and have a sense of their own role as a world citizen;
- respect and value diversity;
- have an understanding of how the world works, economically, politically, socially, culturally, technologically and environmentally;
- are outraged by social injustice;
- participate in and contribute to the community;
- are willing to act in order to make the world more equitable and sustainable;
- take responsibility for their actions.

By adopting the ideas and proposals in this book, teachers themselves will become global citizens, valuing diversity and tackling injustice. Young (2002: 8) stresses that global citizenship is not another subject area, but a way of teaching which can be integrated into existing practices in schools. The following outline topics will help teachers to bring the principles of global citizenship into the classroom; they can also be related to the curricula for citizenship education in Scotland, England and Wales. The specified aims for such topics will help teachers to recognise the links with national curricula in English, environmental studies (Scotland), history and geography (England) and personal, social and health education (PSHE). The proposed activities demonstrate how the topics also address a number of the values and dispositions, skills and aptitudes, knowledge and understanding that are detailed in the Curriculum for Education for Citizenship for England and Wales (QCA 1998) and in the consultation paper on Education for Citizenship in Scotland (Learning and Teaching Scotland (LTS) 2000). In all of the proposed activities there is scope for the development of English language across the curriculum and for collaborative learning, both of which are essential to the successful inclusion of bilingual learners in the main-stream curriculum. Although the aims and activities proposed in the outlines that follow are specified for Key Stage 2 (England and Wales) or Primary 5–7 (Scotland), the ideas within the topics could be transferred to other key stages and to a range of subject areas in the secondary school including English, history, geography, modern studies (Scotland) and citizenship (England and Wales).

Where we came from/languages we speak: topic outlines

Where We Came From/Languages We Speak: KS2 (England and Wales) P5–7 (Scotland)

Aims	Links with National Curriculum	Links with 5–14 Guidelines
To help pupils to acknowledge diversity and to understand the reasons (economic, social, legal) for migration/linguistic variation	Geographical Enquiry and Skills – Knowledge and Understanding of Places English – Language Variation	Environmental Studies – People and Place, People in Society, People in the Past English Language – Knowledge about Language
To encourage the use of reading for information and functional writing in a meaningful context	English – Reading for Information, Composition, Range of Purposes for Writing	English Language – Reading for Information, Functional Writing, Awareness of Genre
To enable pupils to value their own and each other's cultural and linguistic heritage	Personal, Social and Health Education – Developing good relationships and respecting the differences between people	Personal and Social Development – Interpersonal relationships

Aims	Links with National Curriculum	Links with 5–14 Guidelines
To utilise pupils' existing skills in data collection organisation and presentation	Geographical Enquiry and Skills Historical Enquiry and Skills	Environmental Studies – Social studies skills People in the Past – Change and Continuity, Cause and Effect
To enable the pupils to collaborate in the production of a resource of value to the school community	English – Speaking, group discussion and interaction Art and Design – Exploring and developing ideas Personal, Social and Health Education – Developing confidence and responsibility and making the most of their abilities	English Language – Audience awareness Environmental Studies – Social studies skills Expressive Arts: Art, Music and Drama may be incorporated Personal and Social Development – Inter-personal relationships

Activities	Links with Education for Citizenship values and dispositions (V/D), skills and aptitudes (S/A), knowledge and understanding (K/U)
• **Oral History**: pupils collaborate to devise interview schedules for use with parents, grandparents and carers around questions such as Where were you born? How many houses have you lived in? Why did you move? Did any of your family emigrate? / for use with all family members re languages spoken, read, learned at school, listened to or watched, understood	• Disposition to work with and for others (V/D) • Individual initiative and effort (V/D) • Ability to cooperate and work effectively with others (S/A) • Ability to consider and appreciate the experience and perspectives of others (S/A) • Ability to develop a problem-solving approach (S/A) • Ability to look for fresh evidence (S/A) • Nature of diversity (K/U) • Nature of social, moral and political challenges faced by individuals and communities (K/U) • Economic system as it relates to individuals and communities (K/U)

Activities	Links with Education for Citizenship values and dispositions (V/D), skills and aptitudes (S/A), knowledge and understanding (K/U)
• **Mapping**: on large-scale maps of the UK, Europe and the world, pupils map the different places their ancestors have travelled from/the roots of the languages used by the families of pupils in the class	Similar links as for the Oral History activity plus: • Willingness to be open to changing one's opinions and attitudes in the light of discussion and evidence (V/D) • The nature of democratic communities, including how they function and change (K/U)
• **Functional Writing**: pupils produce charts to show the diversity of origins of the families in their class; posters to invite people to come to the UK to work; reports on economic and social reasons for migration/samples of written languages used by families within the class, multilingual dictionaries	Similar links as for the above activities plus: • Ability to make a reasoned argument both verbally and in writing (S/A)
• **Reading for Information**: pupils use a range of sources, including the Internet, to research immigration and emigration statistics/range of scripts. Pupils collect samples of range of scripts within the environment	Similar links as for the above activities plus: • Ability to use modern media and technology critically to gather information (S/A)
• **Environmental exploration** of evidence of immigration/linguistic diversity in the local community. This could be done in conjunction with organised walks in Black History month	Similar links as for the above activities plus: • A critical approach to evidence put before one (S/A)
• **Songs** of migration/songs and rhymes in different languages. In addition to collecting and/or learning such songs and rhymes, there should be discussion about the sentiments expressed/the range of ways of expressing meaning	Similar links as for the above activities plus: • Ability to tolerate other viewpoints (S/A)

Activities	Links with Education for Citizenship values and dispositions (V/D), skills and aptitudes (S/A), knowledge and understanding (K/U)
• **Assembly or exhibition** at the end of the topic on the subject of Where We Came From/Languages We Speak	As this activity will be the result of all the above work, pupils should be able to demonstrate development in all the areas of citizenship identified

CHAPTER 5

Learning Support or Language Support?

As mentioned in Chapter 1, Gillborn and Gipps (1996) found that problems with language can sometimes be misinterpreted as indicative of deeper seated learning difficulties, resulting in inappropriate assessment or even exclusion.

It is important to note that this misinterpretation may result from the fact that there is no explicit policy for the education of bilingual pupils in many authorities and schools. In my own research (Smyth 2001a), no such policy existed in five of the six authorities investigated, resulting in a lack of direction for schools to formulate a coherent school approach to the education of bilingual pupils. Even where there is reference in schools' policies to the teaching of modern European languages, the language policies frequently ignore the existence of bilingual pupils who are using two languages in their everyday lives.

Constantino (1994) found that mainstream teachers' understandings of second language acquisition were not adequate for meeting the needs of bilingual pupils. The need for mainstream teachers to understand second language acquisition and be equipped with strategies for teaching in multilingual classrooms is not adequately addressed in initial teacher education in either Scotland (Smyth and McKee 1997) or England and Wales (Verma *et al.* 1995). Although knowledge about language and language acquisition and development are addressed in the pre-service education of all teachers in Scotland, it is largely a monolingual English language perspective which is used (Smyth and McKee 1997). It seems possible then, that teachers' practices in relation to bilingual children will be informed by existing practice for monolingual children, which could lead to a deficit view of bilingualism.

Research that I undertook (Smyth 2001a) to discover the influences on mainstream teachers' practice with bilingual children analysed the cultural models or 'taken-for-granted assumptions' (Gee 1999) which informed their practice when there was little specialist support. This analysis found that the master model which informed teachers' practice in the context being researched was that *bilingual pupils need to become monolingual to succeed.*

This master model 'that helped shape and organize large and important aspects of experience' (Gee 1999) for mainstream teachers led them to subconsciously categorise the bilingual learners as either fitting or not fitting that model, i.e. they did or did not operate monolingually in the dominant language. This distinction and categorisation was commonly used by the teachers to categorise whether the bilingual child in the classroom presented the teacher with any specific challenges. The child's ability in the use of, or literacy in, their first language was not considered by the teachers when describing the bilingual children.

The impact of these subconscious beliefs on teacher practice is discussed in the case studies in this chapter. The challenges faced by teachers in a situation with only a limited policy are discussed and solutions offered to help teachers to better meet the needs of their bilingual pupils.

MEGAN, PRIMARY 4 TEACHER

In an interesting example of this subconscious categorisation of bilingual pupils as fitting or not fitting the master model, Megan (M), a Primary 4 teacher, is talking to a researcher (R). Megan initially indicated she had not worked with any bilingual children prior to Billy, a Cantonese-speaking boy in her class at the time of the research (Billy is referred to as *the first* below):

R   Have you worked with any other bilingual children?
M   *No.*
R   This is the first?
M   *This is the first.* I spent about the first nine years teaching in Glasgow but it was in the schemes, the peripheral schemes, it was X and then Y [names two areas in Glasgow] where you tend to have very few [bilingual children, implied].

Megan later recalled that she had in fact had bilingual children in her class a number of years before in Glasgow (see below). However as their language, i.e. English, *was well established* and they did not require specific support, she had not referred to them when I asked my initial question. Megan has categorised Billy as not fitting the master model, i.e. unlike the previous children, his language (sic) is not well established. This has led to Megan encountering a *challenge* for which she does not feel equipped:

M   I had two Pakistani boys in the class, one Indian girl, one Chinese girl . . . all of these children started school with not a word of English but I had these girls and boys at Primary 6 and by that time *the language was well established*. There were no problems, they didn't need the support. So I have never been in the situation where *I feel this challenge* and I don't really feel as though . . . I still feel that I don't have the background.

(Note: Primary 4 is the fourth year of primary education in Scotland. The italics highlight significant points discussed in the text.)

Issues

The substitution of the word 'language' for 'English language' was one which was made by a number of the teachers working in the monolingual context under investigation.

All the teachers I interviewed for the purposes of my research expressed a desire for the children to fit in and not feel isolated, but when this aim was analysed in the light of the interviews and the teachers' practices it seemed that in order to fit in, the onus was on the child to operate monolingually in English. This master model has been alluded to in other work related to the education of bilingual children (Biggs and Edwards 1994) although not explicitly named or explained. The master model was not only held by individual teachers but is embedded in education provision in the UK, which at the time of writing does not consider the needs of bilingual pupils in national policy statements.

Possible solutions

There is no doubt that being faced with a child in your classroom who does not share the language of the classroom is a daunting and challenging experience for teachers who wish to help all their pupils to achieve to the best of their ability. Solutions suggested in previous chapters will help in this situation, particularly:

- Information gathering and initial targets   Chapter 1
- Teaching skills and concerns audit   Chapter 2
- Collaborative group work strategies   Chapter 2, elaborated in Chapter 7
- Parental liaison, especially concerning homework   Chapter 3
- Assessing what the pupil can do and knows   Chapter 4
- Involving the child in global citizenship topics   Chapter 4

In addition to these initial solutions however, the teacher will require to take account of the language content of his or her teaching. This chapter will describe how to consider language in the process of planning teaching across the curriculum. Before this discussion however, three further case studies will be used to demonstrate the confusions that may arise for teachers when they are working in the absence of a coherent policy.

JENNA, PRIMARY 2 TEACHER

Jenna (J) compared Jo, a bilingual pupil in her class, to her Chinese-speaking friend, whose English language acquisition she believed had been hindered by not having anyone to speak English to outside the school setting:

J   My best friend's Chinese and it's Cantonese they speak at home and in the restaurant and her English is dreadful. Her grammar, she talks about 'too many cheese' instead of too much cheese. Her grammar is not good at all. They speak it at home and I think *she had to go to the Learning Unit* as well so I don't know, *it can depend on the child* 'cos she has cousins as well that are super brains and they were away to university at 16. I think *it depends on how clever the child is* and how quickly they can pick up [English, implied] and also she was the oldest so she didn't have anyone speaking English at all, whereas her younger brother and her younger sister are much more fluent.

(Note: Primary 2 is the second year of primary education in Scotland. The italics highlight significant points discussed in the text.)

Issues

Several of the teachers interviewed in my research explicitly viewed the bilingual pupil's progress as being evidenced only when the child made more use of English.

Jenna referred to her friend attending the *Learning Unit*. By this she meant the Bilingual Support Unit, which, at the time of the research, Jo attended four mornings a week. Jenna frequently referred to this provision as learning support rather than language support, indicating her belief that bilingual children who did not fit into the monolingual requirement of the system required remedial learning support. Her suggestion that ability depended on the child ('I think *it depends on how clever the child is*') implies that responsibility for a bilingual pupil's success does not lie with the school.

Possible solutions

Jenna expressed a desire to visit the Bilingual Support Unit to see how they catered for Jo. It is unfortunate that as a mainstream teacher with a bilingual pupil in her class she has not been enabled to discuss the specialist support which is offered to Jo, and which may have helped her to recognise the distinction between language support and learning support. Jenna also needs to be assisted with ways of assessing Jo's progress which are not dependent on English language. These might include:

- assessing his ability to collaborate with others in the solution of problems, using activities such as those presented in Chapter 7;
- offering him tasks to complete in, for example, mathematics, which do not involve considerable English language demands; with the exception of the National Curriculum for English/5–14 Guidelines for English Language, there is no general requirement for children to demonstrate their abilities solely in English;
- presenting tasks in a multicultural/multilingual context, taking into account the different cultural experiences that Jo may have compared with his monolingual classmates (as for Mark in Chapter 3).

In Chapter 1, Mary was surprised to hear Mai Ye, a pupil whom she had known for two years, speak to her younger sister, Su Lin, in Cantonese. It may be that one of the reasons why teachers hold onto the master model of monolingualism is that they feel so unaware themselves of their bilingual pupils' home languages and cultures. This lack of awareness was acknowledged by a number of the teachers.

GWEN, PRIMARY 5 TEACHER

At the start of the academic year 1998–1999, the authority in which Gwen (G) and Mary (Chapter 1) taught appointed one Chinese bilingual assistant to work in a number of schools. This bilingual assistant, Mrs Ho, saw Mai Ye once a fortnight for an hour. Gwen discussed this support with me (R) in a later interview, although she acknowledged that she herself still did not know what Mai Ye's first language was:

G   She [Mrs Ho] takes her out and works with her because of the fact that they're working with you know in Chinese, well I'm not sure if it's Cantonese or what it is they're working in. You see there you are again, I'm not absolutely sure what the . . . which one of the languages it is that Mai Ye uses.

R   You were saying that if there's something that you feel Mai Ye's really stuck with you leave it to Mrs Ho . . .

G   Well I would obviously teaching wise, educationally, if there are things that have to get done by me then they get done by me but if I feel that there's something that she would, that I would like to spend a lot of time with or have somebody spend time with then I would ask Mrs Ho to work with her and I would have to spend some time with her and again, there you are, we're into this business of how do you manage your support, where do you get the time to liaise with them and juggle and this is another aspect of the difficulties. The support staff are there, there's no question of that, it's just how do we use them to our best advantage and they're not mind readers.

R   No, and as you said Mrs Ho is not a teacher . . .

G   . . . No, she is a very good eh . . .

R   . . . And you can't really say, right we're at level such and such, go over . . .

G   . . . No, no I can't. I have to try and explain to her what I want and what the point of that particular lesson is. At the moment it's been very simple, it's been things like telling the time so it's been very basic stuff that she would have done with her own children and, you know, I don't imagine she's had any difficulty with that but you know it's going to be an ongoing problem. We can't have *the best of both worlds*; we can't have a Chinese-speaking teacher.

(Note: Primary 5 is the fifth year of primary education in Scotland. The italics highlight significant points discussed in the text.)

Issues

Although Mrs Ho gave Mai Ye a very small amount of support it had alerted Gwen to the possibility of Mai Ye's first language having a place in her education. This suggests there was a change in the master model held by Gwen, i.e. that bilingual pupils need to become monolingual in order to succeed. However, there was no mechanism in place within the school or education authority to provide the guidance and information Gwen would have needed to implement this change. Gwen was aware that Mai Ye had needs which, as a monolingual teacher, she was not able to address, but she had not been helped to acquire the knowledge base to translate her awareness into practice. Gwen expresses a desire that there should be teachers who speak the children's first language and while this would be ideal, the reality is that resources at the current time do not permit this. So what is the monolingual teacher to do? Like Jenna, Gwen tried to make sense of Mai Ye's experience by comparing her to a known adult bilingual (see below) as she did not have experience of working with other bilingual pupils; she expressed a recognition that her many years of teaching monolingual children had not necessarily equipped her to meet Mai Ye's needs:

G   I can only imagine what it must be like trying to work in a language that isn't the language that you're thinking in. I have a friend who is Dutch and she now lives and works here and she says she's fine as long as it's language but she still counts in Dutch.

R   Yes and it's difficult to know how much Mai Ye is trying to work in her home language.

G   So you're conscious that her thought patterns, the way she's picking things up are not necessarily the same as everybody else's, accepting that everybody else has their own variations on a theme as well, but most of us who are working in English will surely be working along similar pathways you know, and as a teacher who has taught as long as I have you are kind of aware of a fair number of the pathways.

Possible solutions

In many situations, the challenges faced by individual teachers cannot be resolved by them acting on an individual basis. Gwen has made new discoveries about the potential of a child's first language for enabling them to learn, but she is unable to do anything about these discoveries in a situation where neither the school nor the authority has a policy for bilingual learners. The school must formulate a policy which has to immediately address the role of Mrs Ho, the bilingual assistant, and how class teachers should work with such staff. Suggestions for the development of an effective policy are included in the final chapter of the book. Having recognised the place of Mai Ye's first language in her education, and acknowledged that there may be different ways of processing different languages, Gwen should, with the support of the newly developed school policy, consider offering Mai Ye opportunities to express herself in her first language, perhaps through the use of a Languages We Speak topic as outlined in Chapter 4.

KAREN, PRIMARY 2 TEACHER

In Whatville Primary, Karen (K) substituted the word 'language' (see below) for English, in common with a number of the other teachers in the research. When talking about Naser (see also case study in Chapter 1), an Urdu-speaking boy whom she taught, she classified his educational needs thus:

K   What his main trouble is really is *lack of language*. I don't think he's as, how shall I put it, not bright as he appears. I talked to his father at parents' night and I asked him how much English was spoken at home because his mother seems to speak Urdu all the time and he said not very much . . . I suggested that perhaps although he's out working a lot he spoke a lot more English in the house . . . he said that quite often he'd say something to Naser in English and he would look as if he didn't understand so he would repeat it in Urdu which I said was fine . . . as long as he gets the English input.

Naser's cousin, Saira, was also in Primary 2 at Whatville and in the same teaching group as Naser for maths and language work. Karen had mentioned that in the early stages of primary school Saira used to take responsibility for Naser. I was interested to know if the teachers enabled the two bilingual pupils to work together:

R   Do him and Saira do they work together at all now?
K   Not really, not really, he's kind of on his own now. The children are quite helpful to him. I explained at one point that it was like them being sent to a French school and trying to get on and they're actually quite helpful, they'll sort of say, 'Oh Naser you're doing this' or they'll actually say 'Let me see Naser, oh that's good', obviously taking the cue from me.

In both interviews, and in unrecorded conversations, Karen considered Naser's behaviour to be a cause for concern and she referred frequently to the need to ensure that he conformed:

K   When he first came into the class he stuck out like a sore thumb and you were constantly, constantly at him and he was just naughty all the time.

(Note: Primary 2 is the second year of primary education in Scotland. The italics highlight significant points discussed in the text.)

Issues

Karen considered it to be the parents' responsibility to enable Naser to become fluent in English and to fit into the school norms by speaking to him in English. This is a cultural model which has been discussed further in Chapter 3.

Karen put great emphasis on the need for Naser to fit into the school culture, which, by definition, was a monoculture. Naser had to conform not only with the monolingual norms of the classroom but also, as for all the children, with the cultural norms of classroom behaviour. The expectations as to the nature of these cultural norms were transmitted in English and when Naser did not conform, perhaps because he did not understand, Karen referred to him as sticking out 'like a sore thumb'.

Although Naser was born in Scotland, Karen had explained his needs to the other children in the class as if he was a foreigner who needed encouragement. She could see the benefit of peer support in the class but had not been able to utilise this strategy either to support Naser and Saira's first language or to help them develop English. Karen's view of the bilingual learner as a foreigner was returned to when she discussed her strategies for supporting Naser:

K   I wonder how much he's taking in, I wonder how much of the language he, I mean I always put it two or three different ways and even occasionally resort to pidgin English you know just to make it as simple as possible.

Karen again used 'language' as a synonym for English language, as this was the only language which was recognised in the monolingual institutional context in which she was working. As mentioned in Karen's case study in Chapter 1, she believes in a common-sense view that language has to be simplified in order to be understood by foreigners, a view that has become the dominant influence on her approaches to support for Naser in the absence of any alternative model being presented to her by either school or authority policy, or pre- or in-service teacher education.

In Didmoon Primary, Elsie had also modified her speech to what might be termed pidgin English when talking to Chih Hai: 'No, Mrs G not understand, not speak Chinese' (see Chapter 1). It is an interesting contradiction that while the teachers held a cultural model that suggested the bilingual pupils needed to become monolingual in English, not all the teachers always presented models of fluent English when talking to their bilingual pupils.

From the four case studies presented in this chapter, what appear to be the issues that teachers are concerned about when they consider how to support bilingual learners in the mainstream classroom? What are the differences between learning support and language support and why is it important to make a distinction between them? How can effective English language support be provided for the bilingual child by the mainstream teacher without denying that child's cognitive ability?

Teachers' concerns

- How do you make yourself understood to a child whose home language is not English?
- What is the place of the child's home language in their learning?
- How do you assess the child's comprehension?
- How do you enable the child to be part of the mainstream classroom?

The initial responses to these concerns are addressed throughout this book and will be summarised for reference in the final chapter.

Learning support or language support?

In all of the case studies presented in this chapter – and elsewhere in the book – the teachers concerned have been required to answer these questions by assuming the bilingual child is less able than their monolingual peers: grouping them with less able pupils so that the work is easier; making assessments only where language is not required and by using and encouraging the use of a highly modified English.

Decisions as to how to support bilingual pupils have been based on an understanding of the differentiation principle that can be applied to much learning support – modifying the teacher input or altering the expected pupil output. Meeting the needs of the bilingual pupil requires an understanding of the language demands of the curriculum and attempts to overcome these language demands, rather than a simplification of the input or output.

Why is it important to make a distinction between learning support and language support?

As indicated at the start of this chapter, Gillborn and Gipps (1996) found that problems with language can sometimes be misinterpreted as indicative of deeper seated learning difficulties. This misinterpretation has resulted in inappropriate assessment or even exclusion from classroom life as identified in the CRE (1996) report into special educational needs (SEN) provision. Bilingual children were often over-represented in SEN, being seen as having a language deficit. Falsely premised assumptions at an early stage in education that the bilingual child will be best placed in a lower ability group can have long-lasting effects on the child's educational opportunities. Focusing on a differentiation of the curriculum without explicitly considering the language of tasks can lead to the bilingual child being stuck in a rut of functioning at a low level of cognitive demand, and not being enabled to develop their skills in English language usage.

How can effective English language support be provided for the bilingual child by the mainstream teacher without denying the bilingual child's cognitive ability?

Cummins (1979) proposed a distinction between the basic interpersonal communicative skills (BICS) that would be acquired in a context-embedded linguistic environment and the need for cognitive academic language proficiency (CALP) that could only be fostered in context-reduced academic situations. In proposing this distinction, Cummins (1984: 137–8) wished to stress that heretofore neglected aspects of language proficiency – such as the ability to hypothesise, extrapolate and predict in the second language – are considerably more relevant for students' cognitive and academic progress than are the surface manifestations of proficiency frequently focused on by teachers. Some of the teachers in my study (Smyth 2001a) did make distinctions between types of language skills but were not able, due to lack of guiding policy, to use this distinction in order to plan in any meaningful way for the bilingual pupils. Many of the teachers, working in the context of a monolingual school, were found to focus on surface indicators of language proficiency such as pronunciation and tense usage. Hall (2002) has outlined how to use the Cummins model to help plan support for bilingual pupils and it is not my intention to replicate that discussion here. The Teacher Training Agency (TTA) guidelines on raising the attainment of minority ethnic pupils include a section (TTA 2000: 45–57) on effective language and learning support for pupils for whom English is an additional language. Included in that guidance is the suggestion that 'as well as supporting pupils with the specialist vocabulary associated with subject content, all teachers should also be prepared to teach or comment explicitly on the language forms, functions and structures used to convey that content' (TTA 2000: 47). Gibbons (1991) has discussed the role of a consideration of functions of language in planning support for the bilingual pupil and this will now be considered in relation to specific curriculum contexts. The functions of language are the purposes for which language might be used. In the mainstream school classroom the most common purpose for which language is used by pupils is responding to teacher questions. However, if bilingual children's English language is to be fully developed in the classroom, they need to be given opportunities to hear and use a wide range of other functions of language. This was referred to in the modelling of questions for literacy homework in Chapter 3.

In order to use the functions of language as a planning tool for support for bilingual pupils, it is necessary to consider the functions of language that are required in order for pupils to fully participate across the curriculum, as indicated in Table 5.1. As can be seen, cognitive academic language skills are required across the curriculum. Teachers need to model these forms of language and, importantly, bilingual pupils need to be given plenty of opportunities to put these skills into practice. Without this modelling and opportunity to use the language it will be difficult for the bilingual pupil to develop and extend their use of the English language.

In order to use functions of language as a planning tool for supporting bilingual learners, the teacher also needs to consider the structures which the child may use to express these functions. The structures are the ways of expressing a particular purpose. The range of these ways will vary depending on the age of the child but what is important is that the bilingual child is exposed to new structures and does not always repeat the known ways of expressing ideas. This will now be demonstrated with reference to some of the instances described in Table 5.1.

The consideration of the functions and structures of a lesson as exemplified in Table 5.2 can be used by teachers as a planning format alongside the normal lesson planning. Although teachers, schools and authorities have many different formats for planning, it should be possible to insert two columns related to Functions and Structures onto the end of this planning format. A possible third additional column would be for specialist vocabulary required for the lesson. In the examples in Table 5.2, the specialist vocabulary is recorded in brackets for the PE and art lessons. A photocopiable format for adding to curriculum planning is provided at the end of this chapter. A final column has been added to this planning format, headed Assessment notes. Here the teacher may record comments drawn from informal assessment through observation and listening as to whether the bilingual pupils are using the targeted functions and structures. This will aid in subsequent planning. A sample of what may be recorded here is suggested in Table 5.3 in relation to the lessons planned in Table 5.1.

Table 5.1 Functions of language across the curriculum

Stage	Curriculum area	Activity	Functions of language which may be used
Primary 1/Year 1	Maths	Group sorting objects into heavy and light	Comparing, classifying, agreeing, disagreeing, describing
Primary 3/Year 3	People in the Past/History	Class discussion reporting findings of what games their grannies played when their age	Enquiring, questioning, explaining, describing, reporting
Primary 4/Year 4	PE	Groups to plan and implement sequences of rolling movements	Planning, giving instructions, evaluating, suggesting, expressing position, explaining
Primary 5/Year 5	Science	Group testing waterproof qualities of materials and recording results	Comparing, classifying, evaluating, identifying, hypothesising, planning, predicting, reporting
Primary 7/Year 7	People and Place/Geography	Discussion about the destruction of rainforests and what might happen in the future	Hypothesising, inferring, predicting, speculating, suggesting, wishing
Secondary 2/Year 9	Art	Reporting on a visit to a gallery	Expressing likes and dislikes, comparing, evaluating, agreeing and disagreeing, identifying
Secondary 4/Year 11	Modern Studies/Citizenship	Planning a visit to parliament	Asking for permission, planning, suggesting, asking for directions

Table 5.2 Structures of language across the curriculum

Stage	Curriculum area	Activity	Functions of language which may be used	Structures of language which may be used
Primary 4/Year 4	PE	Groups to plan and implement sequences of movement involving rolling	Planning, giving instructions, evaluating, suggesting, expressing position, explaining	I think we should . . . . If you do a (forward roll) I could do a . . . . That's better than . . . . Maybe we could . . . . I'll stand behind . . . . You need to start here.
Secondary 2/Year 9	Art	Reporting on a visit to a gallery	Expressing likes and dislikes, comparing, evaluating, agreeing and disagreeing, identifying	My favourite was . . . . The (Van Gogh) was more (colourful) than the . . . . I didn't think the (Picasso) was as (realistic) as the . . .

Table 5.3 Specialist vocabulary and assessment of language use

Functions of language which may be used	Structures of language which may be used	Specialist vocabulary	Assessment notes
Planning, giving instructions, evaluating, suggesting, expressing position, explaining	I think we should . . . . If you do a (forward roll) I could do a . . . . That's better because . . . . Maybe we could . . . . I'll stand behind . . . . You need to start here.	Forward, backward, sideways roll Neater, tidier Behind, beside, in front of	Imran used a lot of specialist vocabulary to explain what he would do and to describe positions but he did not give instructions to the others or evaluate any of the movements
Expressing likes and dislikes, comparing, evaluating, agreeing and disagreeing, identifying	My favourite was . . . . The (Van Gogh) was more (colourful) than the . . . . I didn't think the (Picasso) was as (realistic) as the	Names of artists, paintings Colourful, bright, realistic, surreal	Yoshiko expressed her likes and dislikes but did not compare any of the paintings with each other

Although this extra planning may seem an onerous additional burden, not only will the explicit consideration given to functions and structures of language across the curriculum enhance the learning of the bilingual pupil but all the pupils in the class will be given the opportunity to extend their language usage, and the resultant teaching will be more rewarding. Stage or department groups of teachers can work together on such planning which will be valuable professional development on the role of language in learning.

Planning language support across the curriculum

Curricular area	Lesson	Activities	Functions of language which may be used	Structures of language which may be used	Specialist vocabulary	Assessment notes

CHAPTER 6

Bilingual Pupils Making Sense of a Monolingual Curriculum

The pupils under discussion in this book are all bilingual. Much of the specific educational provision for such pupils in the UK, e.g. through the Ethnic Minority Achievement Grant in England and Wales, is referred to by terms such as bilingual support. Are bilingual children in the UK therefore receiving bilingual education? Cazden and Snow (1990: 4) suggest that bilingual education is a simple label for a complex phenomenon. The range of educational responses to the needs of language minority children in the UK has been described in other chapters of this book. In the context used by many Anglo-American writers on the subject of bilingual education, the term suggests that two languages are used as the medium of instruction. However, most of the education received by language minority children in the UK is through the medium of English, the majority language, only.

In their study of the academic achievement of 700,000 bilingual pupils in five school districts of the US over a 14-year period, Thomas and Collier found (1997: 15) that 'the first predictor of long-term school success (for language minority students) is cognitively complex on-grade level academic instruction through students' first language for as long as possible and cognitively complex on-grade level academic instruction through the second language (English) for part of the school day'.

What are the forms of education for bilingual pupils in the UK?

As has been indicated, such practice is not the situation for most bilingual pupils in the UK who receive all their teaching through the medium of English, their second, or additional language. It can be difficult to know what is the best form of provision for bilingual pupils when the ideal as identified by Thomas and Collier does not exist in the UK.

Several writers have attempted to categorise forms of education for bilingual pupils to try to make the term less complex and ambiguous. Mackey (1970) proposed 90 different forms of bilingual education, depending on the language(s) of the home, the curriculum and the community, and the relative status of the languages. The complexity of Mackey's categorisation has been criticised by Skutnabb-Kangas (1981), who suggested that many of his distinctions are difficult to distinguish and that he fails to clarify whether he is referring to individuals or systems. However, in terms of the four headings proposed by Mackey, it can be noted that in the UK the language of the curriculum is English and that in relation to the many home languages of the bilingual pupils, English is viewed as being of higher status. Mackey's categorisation does not consider the linguistic outcome of educational programmes for bilingual children.

Fishman's (1976) categorisation considers the linguistic aims of a programme as the central feature, i.e. whether the education aims to maintain and develop the minority language or utilise it only as a tool to developing full competence in the majority language. This categorisation is useful in considering planned provision for bilingual children in which two languages are used as the medium of instruction. It is not useful in the context of the majority of schools in the UK where English alone is the medium of instruction, and the maintenance and development of the minority language is given very little consideration.

Baker's (1996: 175) ten point classification of bilingual education is derived from a consideration of the British context. He further categorises the ten proposed types of education for bilingual children as being weak or strong in promoting bilingualism.

As already stated, the language of the classroom for most children in UK schools is the majority language (English). Interviews I conducted with teachers in my research suggest that many of the stated educational aims of the teachers for bilingual children were related to socialising them to enable full participation in the monolingual school community. Observation of classroom practice also conducted for this research showed evidence of linguistic aims of monolingualism in the majority language. These three features – the language of the classroom, the educational and the linguistic aims – reflect an overall aim in the schools for assimilation of the bilingual child linguistically and culturally into the majority language and culture. Together, these aims are concordant with Baker's submersion type of education for bilingual children, which he classifies as the weakest form of education in terms of promoting bilingualism.

Longitudinal research by Thomas and Collier (1997) considered the effectiveness of six forms of educational provision for the achievement of bilingual learners who started education with little English. The six forms of programme analysed had different instructional intentions. The most favourable programmes were those that provided maintenance of the home language alongside development of the second language, while the programmes with the least favourable results and prognosis for the academic achievement of bilingual pupils were those that focused on English only, whether by withdrawal or in the classroom. These latter forms of support are the ones which prevail in the UK context.

In a situation where bilingual pupils are being educated by a means which has been shown by the Thomas and Collier research likely to be the least favourable for their educational achievement, what strategies do the pupils adopt in order to achieve? The following case studies, drawn from my research, will demonstrate the apparent difficulties encountered by bilingual pupils and some of the strategies used by the children to overcome the difficulties. The children's responses will then be discussed.

SAIMA, AGE 6

In Primary 2 in Whatville Primary, Karen, the class teacher was talking to another member of staff while the children (six years old) were working individually on written English language tasks. Saima, a Punjabi-speaking girl, was completing a task in a phonics workbook and seemed to be having difficulty. The task involved reading three-letter words and drawing a representation of the word. The three words on the page were *rag*, *bug* and *hat*. Karen had told the children 'they are all soundy words today'. Saima had drawn a hat but then came to me, in the absence of Karen, and told me *'I can't read rag and bug'*.

(*Note: Primary 2 is the second year of primary education in Scotland. The italics highlight significant points discussed in the text.*)

Difficulties

Saima phonically decoded, or sounded out the words, as the task required but she clearly did not know the meaning of the words 'rag' and 'bug'. Comprehension of the vocabulary was required in order to complete the task by drawing pictures of a rag and a bug.

Strategies

In order to overcome her difficulties, Saima asked an adult for assistance with the comprehension of the words by saying to me 'I can't read rag and bug'.

Implications

Saima appeared to have a more developed understanding of the nature of reading than the textbook – or perhaps the class teacher – in that she knew reading had to involve understanding and not merely decoding. When the teacher marked the work after the task she could only assess whether or not Saima had decoded. A failure to complete the required drawings would suggest to the teacher that the child had failed on this task rather than recognising the child's understanding of the complexity of reading. Conversely, if Saima completed the task having received help with the vocabulary comprehension from an adult other than the teacher, the teacher would not know of Saima's language needs. The form which Saima chose to use to request help – 'I can't read rag and bug' – is also significant as it is indicative of Saima not being able to use a more usual formulation of this request such as 'What do rag and bug mean?'

ASIF, AGE 9

Fiona is a peripatetic English as an Additional Language (EAL) teacher who visits each of her allocated primary schools twice a week. Because the education authority has minimal provision but no policy for bilingual learners, each school decides how the EAL teacher will be utilised. In Whatville Primary, Fiona is required to withdraw the bilingual pupils and give them support with whatever the class teacher decides. On the one occasion I observed Fiona working with Asif, a Punjabi-speaking boy. The class teacher had given Fiona a copy of the Writing National Test and asked her to prepare it with him. She had not seen this test before and had difficulty knowing how to support Asif with a decontextualised piece of imaginative writing entitled 'Down the Plughole'.

The test was going to be taken by the group the next day under exam conditions and Ellen (the class teacher) wanted Fiona to help Asif with the planning of the story. The test papers incorporate a planning page on which children are intended to write notes in response to content questions before writing the complete story. In this case the planning questions were:

Where is the plughole?
How did the person get into it?
What did the person see?
How did the person feel?
What happened?
How does your story end?

Fiona (F) started the session with Asif (A) by asking him the first question without any discussion of the purpose of the task or the possible genre of the story:

F   Where is the plughole?
A   Sink, bath.
F   Where are you – bath or sink?
A   Bath.
F   Write that down.
(A wrote 'bath'.)

F Why are you in the bath?
A To do a bath.
F Are you dirty or has something happened to get you dirty?
A 'Cos I'm dirty.
F What have you done to make you dirty?
A Fallen in mud.
F Write that down. F – A – L – L – E – N.
(A wrote 'fallen'.)
F What is the sentence you'd write? Make a sentence using these two
   bits.
A I was playing in mud then I fallen then I went in my house then I had
   a bath.
F Write something like that.

The interaction continued in this way with Fiona going through the planning questions, Asif responding and Fiona helping him to write responses which it was
intended he would use the next day to write the story.

Difficulties

The notes which Asif has made on his planning sheet will not help him to write
an imaginative story. The sentence he wrote 'I was playing in mud then I fallen
then I went in my house then I had a bath' reads as a piece of personal writing
rather than imaginative. This form of writing has resulted directly from Fiona's use
of 'you'. It is not apparent that Asif understands the difference between personal
and imaginative writing. Ways of helping Asif to understand this distinction are
discussed at the end of this section along with a discussion of the role of the EAL
teacher and support for the planning of writing.

Strategies

In this case study it would appear that Asif tried very hard to answer the teacher's
questions, but the directed approach taken to the task by Fiona did not allow him
to overcome the difficulties identified above in relation to the purpose of planning
or imaginative writing.

Implications

This is an Imaginative Writing test, but at no point did Fiona take the opportunity to discuss the nature of imaginative writing with Asif. In this way, Asif's creativity was stifled.

The role, which had been ascribed to the EAL teacher by the school, was to enable the bilingual child to operate in the context of the monolingual assessment procedures. At the end of this session Asif was expected to have planning notes, so Fiona helped him to achieve these, thereby missing the opportunity to support his knowledge about language which might enable him to write more successfully and independently in future. The cultural model that Asif has learning deficiencies which require remediation is resulting in a self-fulfilling prophecy. On the occasion described in the above case study, Asif was extracted from the class for 45 minutes while the rest of his group were doing practical work on symmetry. Anna, the teacher responsible for Asif's maths group, was concerned that Asif would miss this teaching and asked Fiona if she would cover it with him another time, to which Fiona agreed. In this way, the EAL teacher was being used by the school to plug gaps in learning rather than to plan coordinated and targeted language support for Asif. He missed out on class work when he was withdrawn for this support by the EAL teacher, resulting in more learning needs.

The personal/imaginative writing distinction

The bilingual learner needs to know the functions and structures of language required for different styles of writing. The planning format provided at the end of Chapter 5 will be useful for identifying the specific language demands of the genres. The functions, structures and vocabulary identified in Table 6.1 are only a small proportion of those needed for successful personal and imaginative writing. The language required will depend on the task as well as on the age of the learner.

It is important that the teacher should consider in advance what the required language will be and models this for the child. This modelling needs to be done by reading aloud from a range of genres as well as through class writing and focused questions which use the target language, for example, *How would you feel if you were . . . ?* (personal) *What do you think it might be like (down the plughole)? What might happen if . . . ?* The use of *might* in these latter two questions will encourage imaginative thought and response, whereas questions such as *Are you dirty* or *Has something happened to get you dirty?* used by Fiona, will encourage a personal response.

Table 6.1   The language of personal and imaginative writing

Activities	Functions of language which may be used	Structures of language which may be used	Specialist vocabulary
Personal writing	Expressing emotion and attitudes, expressing a personal response	Use of first person narrative, I felt . . . I know . . . I think . . . I liked the way . . .	Words expressing feelings
Imaginative writing	Describing characters and setting, narrating	Once upon a time As (cold) as (ice)	Range of adjectives and adverbs, similes

Bilingual learners and the planning of writing

The importance of planning writing has been well documented (Graves 1983; Styles 1989). Planning is built into the National Tests for Writing in the UK, and is particularly important for the bilingual child, not only to help them think about the sequence and content of their work but also to enable the teacher to assess if the child may need support with particular functions, structures and vocabulary. The planning of writing, however, is a skill in itself which needs to be taught. The purpose and process of the plan need to explained and modelled. The teacher should show how s/he approaches the planning of a piece of writing by modelling the planning process to a group or the whole class using a large sheet of paper and a marker. Depending on the type of writing, questions such as *Who is in the story? Where does the story take place? What happens in the story?* will be written on the paper. The teacher should record the characters, setting and plot under these questions, focusing on using the terms 'characters', 'setting' and 'plot'. Sub-questions may then also be recorded on the paper such as *How does the story begin? Describe the main characters/setting; How does the story end?*

On a separate sheet of paper, the teacher should then demonstrate the transition from the plan to the actual story, including the rejection of some of the originally planned ideas and the addition of new ones. This is important so that the child does not believe the plan to be rigid.

For bilingual children particularly, the use of writing partners and/or collaborative planning will be important. The children may work in a group to brainstorm ideas at the planning stage to extend the range of ideas and vocabulary used. They can then individually plan their own work using some of the group ideas. With a partner, the children can question each other about how they will move from one section of the plot to the next, how they will introduce the different characters, how they will use description to build up tension etc.

The role of the EAL teacher

In the case study above, neither Asif nor the class teacher benefited from the presence of the EAL teacher, nor was any job satisfaction gained by the EAL teacher herself. All schools with bilingual pupils – but particularly those where additional support is peripatetic – need to have a policy that establishes how the additional support for bilingual learners will be used. Where the teacher is peripatetic, as in Fiona's situation, it may be that the best use of the EAL teacher is to offer advice and guidance to the class and subject teachers on how to support the bilingual children, rather than to work directly with the pupils themselves. This will have a more lasting impact on the ability of the bilingual pupils to access the curriculum.

JO, AGE 6

Jo, a Chinese-speaking boy, is in Primary 2 at North Primary School. He attends mainstream school in the morning for language and maths and goes four afternoons a week to an off-site Language Support Centre. While at the Centre, Jo completes any homework he has from the mainstream class.

During the language programme in the class, the children are given four independent, individual written tasks, during which time the class teacher intends to 'hear' all the children reading from their commercial reading text. During my research I observed the children working on the language programme The first task involved copying the day's spelling word ('if') six times into homework jotters. The spelling of this word was then expected to be learned at home and a sentence containing 'if' written into the jotters at home. Jo wrote 'it' six times into his jotter.

The third task was a workbook connected to the Link-Up reading scheme (Holmes McDougall). The workbook directed the child to turn to the appropriate page of the textbook. However the workbook page Jo had to complete did not correspond to the textbook he was currently using, so he did not have the appropriate text in front of him. He therefore had difficulty with the comprehension tasks which required him to fill in gaps in sentences with the appropriate word. The italics below indicate Jo's written responses:

> Nicky liked to eat *banana*
> Nicky took the *banana* off the banana.

[The postman wore* a _____ on his head.]

The boy next to Jo asked me 'Do you know that * word?' I told him, 'wore'. The boy then read out 'The policewoman (sic) wore a coat?' and wrote 'cout' in the space.

Jo then copied this boy's answer, resulting in

The postman wore a *cout* on his head.

Jo then put this workbook away and went to the teacher's desk with his Link-Up text-book to read aloud.

(Note: Primary 2 is the second year of primary education in Scotland.)

Difficulties

Jo copied the homework incorrectly from the blackboard, possibly due to careless-ness, but it is likely that he wrote *it* rather than *if* because the former was a more familiar word. As Jo had only been using English since he came to school 18 months earlier, it is likely that he does not yet use or have familiarity with the con-ditional form needed to recognise the letters *i* and *f* as a word.

It is not surprising that Jo had difficulties with the workbook task as he did not have the text in front of him to enable completion of the task. The character of Nicky, introduced in the previous book, is a monkey, who does, in fact, eat bananas. Jo completes this first sentence from his prior knowledge of the charac-ter. However, he uses the singular form 'banana' rather than the grammatically cor-rect plural form. His chosen words for completion of the next two sentences indi-cate that he has not read to the end of the sentences and understood the meaning of what he has written.

Strategies

In the first case, Jo has chosen a known word *it* because he did not know the word *if*. This is a creative substitution to overcome his difficulty. With regard to the workbook task, Jo has relied on his memory for the first sentence. The correct word to fill the second space is 'skin' but as Jo did not know the word he used the known word *banana*. As described, in the third sentence, Jo copied the wrong answer from the boy next to him.

Implications

The class teacher will not have seen the error in Jo's homework jotter until the next day, by which time he will have done his homework at the Bilingual Support Unit where the error will not be noticed as there is no daily contact between the school and the Unit. Given the pressures on the class teacher's time, it is unlikely that this error will be investigated and Jo's non-use of the conditional form will continue.

Jo's workbook task would not be marked until after he had left the school to go to the Bilingual Support Unit. Jenna, the class teacher, would see he had made errors but would not be able to assess the reasons for these errors. Not only the school curriculum but also the work organisation which Jenna, a new teacher, has encountered in the school, leaves her little room to question the cultural model – that as a bilingual child, Jo has learning difficulties. This in turn offers little opportunity for Jo to progress. It could be that the tasks on this particular day resulted in specific errors which did not normally occur; when I asked Jenna about his comprehension she commented that his workbook answers were usually correct:

> R   What about his reading? Do you think he understands what he's reading?
> J   I think [pause] I'm not sure 'cos he doesn't answer the questions [orally], *if we do the reading workbook then I suppose he must understand it up to a point because it's correct and that's really all I've got to go on for that.* The learning support . . . the bilingual unit, they do his reading at night, so . . .

The support required for Jo to succeed was framed by Jenna in terms of monolingual English literacy practices and processes.

> R   But what do you think he might need help with?
> J   [pause] maybe, probably his reading and phonics.

The specific needs of the bilingual child were not assessed or addressed in relation to the tasks which Jenna assumed he would be able to complete.

As was discussed in Chapter 5, the child not completing the task in the way the teacher expects may lead the teacher to underestimate his/her ability, resulting in the bilingual child being placed in an inappropriate learning group. The difficulty faced by the bilingual child may be because of specific language functions, structures or vocabulary not being in place. In order to give the bilingual child the best possible opportunity to achieve, the teacher needs to be able to assess the language demands of any particular task and to analyse the responses made by the child to evaluate possible reasons for error. This requires the use of the planning format in Chapter 5. The tasks which Jo had to complete during this language session did not lead to any development of his English language use. Many of the strategies proposed by the National Literacy Strategy would be far preferable to the language programme presented in this case study, but unfortunately this type of decontextualised and unsupported work is not atypical in an education system with large classes and increasing demands on teachers.

Each of the case studies presented in this chapter has involved bilingual children struggling with a monolingual curriculum and teachers not knowing the reasons for their difficulties. The following framework – presented first in a completed format related to Asif (see case study in this chapter) and then in a blank photocopiable format – will help the class or subject teacher to assess the child's work, to analyse the reasons for these errors and to plan support for overcoming the difficulties.

Table 6.2   Planning and assessing Asif's learning

Name: Asif	Date:
What is the learning planned?	Planning for National Test in Imaginative Writing
What will the child do to show s/he has successfully achieved the learning?	Record responses to planning questions which will help in the writing of a story
What exactly is the task?	Answer planning question
What functions of language does the child require to use in order to achieve the learning?	Describing; explaining; speculating; sequencing
What is the problem with what s/he has done?	Limited unimaginative responses Responses don't fit planning questions Responses in 1st person Responses do not seem a support for writing an imaginative story
What misunderstandings might this indicate on the child's part?	Child does not know purpose of planning and does not realise this is meant to be an imaginative piece of writing Perhaps distinction between personal and imaginative writing is not clear
What support could be given to enable the child to achieve the learning?	Read and discuss examples of personal and imaginative writing; teach and model planning

Planning and assessment of bilingual pupils' learning

Name:	Date:
What is the learning planned?	
What will the child do to show s/he has successfully achieved the learning?	
What exactly is the task?	
What functions of language does the child require to use in order to achieve the learning?	
What is the problem with what s/he has done?	
What misunderstandings might this indicate on the child's part?	
What support could be given to enable the child to achieve the learning?	

CHAPTER 7

Overcoming the Challenges

Teaching bilingual children is rewarding and exciting. Watching a child acquiring the English necessary to express him/herself in your classroom can give teachers a wonderful sense of achievement. Knowing that you have the responsibility for enabling a bilingual child to access a monolingual curriculum can be daunting however. As Megan commented in Chapter 5, 'I feel this challenge and I don't have the background'. One of the aims of this book has been to give mainstream teachers some of the background necessary to begin to overcome that challenge, but there will always be further questions as every teacher wants to do the best for every child and every child is different. This chapter will address some of the recurring questions that I have been asked by teachers about teaching bilingual children. The chapter sets out to help teachers to build on their existing knowledge so that they do not view meeting the needs of every bilingual child as a completely new challenge each time. Photocopiable formats are included for analysing the potential difficulties of texts and tasks and for planning collaborative work. Alongside the photocopiable sheets for planning targeted language support across the curriculum in Chapter 5 and the assessment sheets in Chapter 6, these can be used by teachers of any stage and any subject to help meet the needs of bilingual children in their classrooms.

In this first section I shall discuss the questions which most concerned the teachers with whom I worked in my doctoral research. All of these teachers were mainstream primary teachers who had recently begun teaching bilingual pupils. In all cases they did not have a great deal of experience of teaching bilingual pupils and did not have many such pupils in their schools. By presenting in Table 7.1, their relative years of experience and knowledge of bilingual pupils, I hope that readers may be able to identify with the sources of the questions being discussed. This table also identifies some of the reasons why teachers may have these questions about their bilingual pupils.

You will see that my respondents' experience ranges from four to thirty years of teaching. They have a range of teaching qualifications but have in common an almost non-existent input on the needs of bilingual children in their pre-service qualifications. Where any mention was made on their pre-service courses it was, in

Table 7.1 Background of research participants

School	Class	Teacher	Years of service	Number of bilingual children taught previously	Pre-service teacher education (length & type)	Pre-service input on bilingual learners	In-service input on bilingual learners	School written policy on the needs of bilingual learners?	Education authority provision for bilingual children
Kirk Primary	Primary 1/Reception–Year 1	Janet	18	1	3 yrs Diploma in Education (Dip. Ed)	None	None	No	'Bilingual' unit & peripatetic EAL teachers
	Primary 7/Year 6–7	Jackie	13	None	1 yr (PGCE) Postgraduate Certificate in Education	None	None		
North Primary	Primary 2/Year 1–2	Jenna	4	1	4 yrs (B. Ed) Bachelor of Education degree	None	None	Paragraph in Inclusive Education Policy	'Bilingual' unit & peripatetic EAL teachers
	Primary 4/Year 3–4	Megan	20	none in last 12 years; some previously in Glasgow	3 yrs Dip. Ed	None	None		
Nanvale Primary	Primary 1/Reception–Year 1	Morag	11	3	3 yrs Dip. Ed	Some input on cultural difference	None, but involvement in authority guideline preparation	No	'Bilingual' unit & peripatetic EAL teachers
	Primary 5/Year 4–5	Lotty	30	4	3 yrs Dip. Ed	none	None		

Table 7.1 Continued

Fieldhead Primary	Primary 2/Year 1–2	Mary	26	4	3 yrs Dip. Ed	None	None	No	Peripatetic EAL teachers and 1 peripatetic Cantonese class assistant
	Primary 4/Year 3–4	Gwen	30	1	3 yrs Dip. Ed	None	None		
Whatville Primary	Primary 2/Year 1–2	Karen	13	None	1 yr PGCE	None	None	No	Peripatetic teachers
		Morven	25	2	3 yrs Dip. Ed	None	None		
	Primary 5/Year 4–5	Cath	23	2	3 yrs Dip. Ed	None	None		
		Ellen	29	2	3 yrs Dip. Ed	None	Half-day with ESL teacher		
		Claire	10	2	4 yrs B. Ed	some input on cultural difference	None		
		Anna	12	4	3 yrs Dip. Ed	None	None		
Didmoon Primary	Primary 2/Year 1–2	Iona	4	None	4 yrs B. Ed	Bilingualism mentioned in SEN input	None	No	None
	Primary 4/Year 3–4	Pam	12	2	3 yrs Dip. Ed	None	2 days organised for Gaelic medium teachers		
		Elsie	28	None	3 yrs Dip. Ed	None	None		

the case of Morag and Claire, in relation to cultural difference only, rather than to language needs. In the case of Iona, this was in relation to SEN. Both of these issues are of concern, but particularly the latter, especially given the connections that are often assumed, as discussed in Chapter 5, between bilingualism and SEN. It is also worrying that this input was received by one of the more recently qualified teachers. A small-scale study conducted with a colleague in another Scottish teacher education institution (Smyth and McKee 1997) indicated that new teaching graduates believed themselves to be poorly equipped for teaching bilingual children. The students commented that although they had received input on multicultural education they had not been given any guidance on how to teach pupils whose first language was not English. This seems to match with Morag and Claire's experience.

Consideration of the column related to in-service indicates that although all of these teachers are working with bilingual children, they have received virtually no INSET on this issue. The one exception is Pam, who attended a two-day INSET course on bilingualism, which was aimed at the teaching of children through the medium of the Gaelic language. In situations where INSET is driven by curriculum targets it seems increasingly likely that teachers will be unable to attend in-service courses related to the needs of bilingual pupils.

Only one of the six schools in my research mentioned the needs of bilingual pupils in the school handbook. This omission of a section of the pupil population can lead to frustration on the part of teachers who feel they should know how to respond. The one school handbook which did mention bilingual pupils did not offer any guidance as to how their needs might be met or how their bilingualism could benefit their education. Rather, it suggested that, along with disabled pupils and pupils with 'other Special Educational Needs', the school would teach the bilingual pupils.

There is a variety of types of provision for bilingual pupils across the country and even within the same authorities. As can be seen in the table, three of the six authorities in my research had off-site 'bilingual units' in which the bilingual children were educated four half-days per week. This led to the mainstream teachers believing that the bilingual children received the best education in these centres as they were staffed by specialists and that, as generalists with little experience of teaching bilingual children, they could offer little support themselves. It also led to frustrations as the bilingual children inevitably missed large chunks of mainstream education. Five of the six authorities had peripatetic teachers who were spread very thinly over a large number of schools. In some cases these specialist EAL teachers worked in the classroom and in others they withdrew the bilingual children for support. Due to the large number of schools they had to cover there was no time for discussion between the mainstream and the EAL teachers. The consequences of this were highlighted in the discussion about Asif in Chapter 6. One of the authorities had no specific support for bilingual pupils; as a result these pupils were frequently given extra support by the SEN teachers with the resulting confusion as to whether bilingual pupils need language support or learning support. Although my research took place in Scotland, informal discussions with teachers throughout the UK indicate a similar variety of provision, particularly in areas with a small number of bilingual pupils. This variety has not been planned to meet the needs of the bilingual pupils and leads to confusion for mainstream teachers, sending mixed messages as to what is really the best education for such pupils.

This confusion results in teachers having many unanswered questions about how best to meet the needs of bilingual children. Some of the more common questions are identified in the following section, with some suggested answers.

'I don't want to tread on any toes.'

This comment came from a teacher who was rather hesitant about making any particular provision for the bilingual child in her class in case she contravened religious or cultural practices. Mary was concerned about this because the school had not provided her with any information about the child's background. Completion of the form in Chapter 1 will assist with this, but additionally teachers need support to understand some of the religious and cultural beliefs of different groups (see Useful Addresses and Websites). It is also important to liaise closely with the parents as discussed in Chapter 3.

'I want to know more about what the EAL teacher does.'

This comment was made by a number of teachers in the research who believed that if they knew more about how their pupils were supported by the EAL teacher or in the language unit, they would be better equipped to support the children within the classroom on a day-to-day basis.

Darjit was introduced in Chapter 4. He receives support once a week from a peripatetic EAL teacher who withdraws him from the class and works on aspects of English language grammar such as forming plurals, tenses and similes. This work is unrelated to class work, but as the EAL teacher visits eight schools in a week there is never the opportunity for planning with the class teacher as the emphasis is put on contact with the child. Jackie, the class teacher, was not happy with this situation but told me it was school practice:

R   You've not worked with the EAL teacher to discuss work with Darjit at all?
J   No. There's no kind of avenue for working with her because she extracts him and that's what the head teacher likes and that's why we do it.
R   What do you think?
J   I'd rather she came into the class but I'd rather anyone came into the class than have to take him away because he doesn't like it. And all the chit chat and gossip that goes on in the class, well, he might be missing something.

Jackie is very aware of the importance of keeping Darjit in the mainstream classroom, not only for the formal education but also for the interaction with his peers. The difficulties of having no school or authority policies and the support provision being peripatetic have combined here to result in a situation which is not meeting Darjit's needs. A practice has developed in the school and the teachers have not felt able to challenge this. It is important that in this situation a working group, involving mainstream and peripatetic teachers, is established to develop a school policy for, in the first instance, the deployment of peripatetic teachers (as discussed in Chapter 6). This working group could then develop a more detailed policy for bilingual pupils.

Megan and Jenna both expressed a desire to visit the Bilingual Support Unit to see how the teachers there supported the bilingual pupils in the hope that they could transfer some of the strategies to their own teaching. What they were really expressing here was a need to know more about best practice for bilingual pupils. INSET is needed for mainstream teachers throughout the country who are being expected to teach bilingual pupils without an understanding of second language acquisition.

Returning now to the main concerns of the mainstream teachers expressed in Chapter 5, I shall summarise the initial answers, referring back to where these issues have been discussed earlier.

'How do you make yourself understood to a child whose home language is not English?'

- See the response to teaching Sunita, Chapter 2 and Mariela, Chapter 4.
- Use concrete referents and visual aids as often as possible in the initial stages of a child acquiring a new language.
- Enable peer support in the classroom.
- Allow the child time to hear and process the new language.
- Avoid the temptation to use a stilted form of English – use natural language.

'What is the place of the child's home language in their learning?'

- Cummins (1996: 2) summarises the place of children's first language in a powerful quote which explains what schools are doing by ignoring a child's first language: 'when student's language, culture and experience are ignored or excluded in classroom interaction, students are immediately starting from a disadvantage. Everything they have learned about life and the world up to this point is being dismissed as irrelevant to school learning.'
- Bilingual children use two or more languages in their everyday life and this must not be ignored by the school.
- Bilingual pupils bring linguistic knowledge to the classroom which should be shared and valued. See the case studies in Chapter 4.
- Bilingual pupils should be enabled to use their first language to help develop cognitive academic language proficiency in the second language. See the case study on Diljit later in this chapter.

'How do you assess the child's comprehension?'

- Clarify to yourself how the learning will be demonstrated.
- Observe how the child responds to instructions.
- See the planning and assessment format in Chapter 6.
- Refer to the QCA (2000) guidelines.

'How do you enable the child to be part of the mainstream classroom?'

- Carefully plan the input, focusing on the language of lessons. See the discussion in Chapter 5 on using functions of language as a planning tool.
- Plan collaborative activities which will enable the child to participate. See the case study on Wahid below and the planning format for collaborative activities at the end of the chapter.

I will now demonstrate practical solutions to some of the questions asked above through case studies. The first case study involves the planning and use of collaborative group work to support Wahid, a child who is new to using English. The second case study demonstrates how a collaborative approach to a writing task will help May Lee, a child who is showing some consistent grammatical errors in her writing. The third case study indicates how a teacher of English may help Diljit to use her first language, Punjabi, to achieve learning outcomes related to imaginative writing, awareness of genre and audience awareness.

WAHID, AGE 12

Wahid recently arrived in the UK from Somalia as a result of the refugee dispersal programme. He is a bright, sociable child who has very little English. He has been placed in 1st year (Year 7) at secondary school. There are other refugee children in the class but no one else who speaks Somali, his first language. The school wants the refugee children to feel part of the mainstream classes and encourages the planning of collaborative activities where possible. The teachers have identified that Wahid is very able and want to ensure that his limited English does not mean that he cannot participate in learning at his cognitive level. The science class is doing a six-week topic investigating circuits.

Solution

Collaborative tasks will enable Wahid to participate with other children in investigating circuits, e.g. constructing and testing. Wahid should have an active part in the investigations but not be required to produce spoken English. In this situation an ideal group size is three pupils. Wahid should be the experimenter while the other two children take on the roles of observer and recorder. This will ensure that Wahid has a key role to play and is not left out of the learning due to his limited English. The three roles will be mutually interdependent, giving the collaboration a purpose. Task design should include a recording chart and should note the key English vocabulary necessary for the tasks. The teacher will require to pre-teach the key vocabulary and model the method.

Task

The children are given a range of materials from which to construct a circuit and test whether the material conducts electricity, i.e. lights a bulb. Wahid, the experimenter, puts the material (e.g. a nail, a rubber, a plastic ruler, a pencil, a wooden ruler) across the two terminals. The observing pupil says 'yes' or 'no' depending if the bulb lights up and gives Wahid the next material, naming it as s/he does so. The recording pupil marks a tick or a cross beside the material to indicate whether or not it is a conductor of electricity.

The format established for the collaborative science work is one that can be applied across the curriculum. The teacher must ensure that the bilingual child who is new to English has an important role to play in the task but is not required to produce any spoken English. The bilingual child should have the opportunity to hear the other pupils using the language necessary for comprehension of the task. The teacher should ensure that written instructions are understood.

Collaboration is an important strategy regardless of the English language abilities of the bilingual child. Collaboration for another purpose, in another curricular area and for a pupil with more English is examined in the next case study.

The photocopiable format at the end of the chapter will assist in the planning of collaborative tasks. It is suggested here that functions and structures of language (see Chapter 5) are considered at this planning stage to enable the teacher to model any target language or ensure that it will be used by the other pupils in the group. In the case of Wahid, above, the target functions will be describing and possibly predicting and speculating. Structures to be used will include, for example, *I think the . . . will conduct electricity because . . .; the . . . won't form a circuit because. . .*

MAY LEE, AGE 10

May Lee speaks Cantonese at home. She has been at school in the UK since Primary 1 (Reception–Year 1). She has made good progress in all areas of the curriculum and is now in Primary 6 (Year 5–6) where she is the only Cantonese-speaking child. As the length of imaginative writing being produced by May Lee has increased, her class teacher has noticed that she has a few repeated difficulties with tense usage and personal pronouns in her writing. For example she consistently uses the *ed* form to represent the past tense: 'I swimmed 10 lengths.' She frequently confuses the masculine and feminine forms: 'Frank ate *her* lunch.'

The class is working on an integrated English and history topic on World War 2. The teacher has planned that May Lee's language group should produce a piece of imaginative writing about the feelings of an evacuee child and wishes to devise support materials for this task to enable May Lee to address the difficulties mentioned above.

Solution

May Lee may be exhibiting these grammatical errors due to the differences between Cantonese and English. Cantonese does not have gender-specific pronouns, nor does the verb form change to indicate tense change, but rather changes the subject form. If neither of these grammatical points have been explicitly taught, May Lee may be using personal pronouns randomly, without understanding the gender-specific nature. She may also be generalising the past tense from the most common *ed* form, applying this to all past tense verbs.

A visual prompt can be devised for May Lee with a female image on one side and a male image on the other side. Under the images can be scribed the relevant personal pronouns – she, her, hers/he, him, his. At this age and stage May Lee could produce this for herself. If it is playing card size she can use it unobtrusively as a prompt when she writes until she is confident in her use of personal pronouns.

Group discussion tasks, writing partners and peer editing will provide good support for May Lee without requiring the teacher to give one-to-one support.

Task

Prior to individual writing, May Lee's group can brainstorm their ideas onto a writing frame with questions such as: *How did the child feel when their parents told them they were going away? What did they decide to pack as well as their clothes? How did they feel when they waved goodbye to their parents at the train station? What was the first thing they did when they got to their new home?*

The questions should carefully be phrased by the class teacher in the past tense to encourage group discussion and recording in the past tense. May Lee should not, at this stage, be asked to record the group answers. The child who does record the plans should be encouraged by the class teacher to use verbs in the planning frame.

May Lee can then read the answers aloud to the group to see if there is anything they think would not be suitable for the set piece of writing. This will give her the chance to hear, read and speak correctly formed past tenses prior to writing.

The children should then be paired with writing partners who will give constructive criticism on the individual writing (taking turns) and help in the editing phase. If this is not normal practice in the classroom, the teacher will require to model the way to respond to another's writing.

When planning this task using the collaborative tasks planning sheet at the end of the chapter, May Lee's role will be, along with the other members of the group, to contribute orally to the brainstorm of ideas. She will also be the reader of the group's ideas, while another member of the group will be the recorder of ideas. The target functions and structures are the past tense expression of feelings and emotions.

The third case study considers how the class teacher may enable a group of Punjabi-speaking pupils to use their first language to tell a story to a group of younger children. This group is very competent in both their first and second language and by using their first language will be given a context for developing their cognitive academic English for purposes of reporting, comparing, contrasting and explaining.

DILJIT, AGE 13

Diljit is in her second year of secondary school. She speaks Punjabi at home. There are four other Punjabi-speaking children in the class and similar numbers in the rest of the classes in the school. They have all been at school in the UK since Primary 1/Reception class.

Diljit's English class is studying a language unit based on fairy and folk tales which is developing the children's imaginative writing, awareness of genre and audience awareness. The teacher has suggested that groups of children should prepare a known fairy story to be performed to the Primary 2 children in the associated primary schools, and has provided a range of anthologies from which the groups should choose a story.

The Punjabi-speaking children have found an English translation of *The Serpent King* in one of the anthologies and have asked if they could work together on it as it is a story their parents have told them. The teacher is keen to enable these children to use their Punjabi in the school context and considers this activity would be an ideal way of doing so. The teacher also sees this as a useful way of involving the parents in their children's education. The teacher and pupils both want their storytelling to be available to all the children in the class, not just the Punjabi-speaking children.

Solution
The group should first devise a storyboard for the key events and characters which they will then use to ensure they include these in their sharing of the story. This should be annotated in English. Parents could be asked to record a telling of the story in Punjabi to help the group to retell the story in Punjabi. The group could then prepare an English translation of the Punjabi story, using the written text as support and comparing their version with the book version. They should be asked to report on the differences and similarities between their translation and the book version. The group could be encouraged to use stick or shadow puppets as visual aids for the non-Punjabi-speaking children. The group should also be asked to report on how they showed awareness of the non-Punjabi-speaking children in their Punjabi presentation of the story.

The next three queries are presented from the point of view of the class teacher, asking how to give immediate support to newly arrived bilingual pupils with little English, how to assess the language demands of curriculum texts and how to help devise a school policy for supporting bilingual pupils.

How do you support newly arrived bilingual pupils with little English?

Imagine you are a mainstream class teacher with a Primary 2 (Year 1–2) class of monolingual English-speaking pupils. Two Cantonese-speaking cousins have just been enrolled in your class. They have recently arrived in the UK from Hong Kong. They have not been at school before and have limited English. They seem to get on well together and you frequently hear them responding to other children in the class in play settings. You do not have a large budget but you wish to enhance your classroom resources to the benefit of these two pupils. A peripatetic EAL teacher visits once a week and works specifically with the two children during the Literacy Hour after the whole-class lesson. The children's parents are interested in their children's education and have visited the school to ask how they can help.

- What resources would you wish to add to your classroom and why?
  As discussed in Chapter 4 in relation to Mark, it will be important to acquire

some culturally relevant materials for the cousins to add to the home corner. A visit to a Chinese supermarket will be valuable for purchasing some inexpensive Chinese utensils.

The cousins need materials that can be used for collaborative activities in the classroom to expose them to the natural English of their peers, so games and large construction kits for imaginative play would be a good investment.

- How can you and the EAL teacher work together most effectively to develop the children's English?

The school management must enable you to have time to discuss focus and approaches with the EAL teacher. S/he needs to know the texts you are working on and you need to know the strategies s/he adopts with the cousins.

The management could provide class cover for you to observe the EAL teacher working with the cousins. This will then give you a focus for discussion as to why the EAL teacher does certain activities and how you can follow these up in the remainder of the week.

- What guidance can you provide for the children's parents to help them develop their literacy?

As discussed in Chapter 3, a parental workshop should be organised to help the parents understand the approaches to literacy taken by the school. It is important that you stress to the parents that they should continue to communicate with the cousins in Cantonese and to read them stories in Cantonese in order to develop their cognitive academic language abilities in their first language. Ask the parents to give you samples of Cantonese script for the writing corner, as discussed in Chapter 4.

'How do you help the bilingual child to access complex written texts?'

The written demands of curriculum materials may result in bilingual pupils being placed in lower ability groups than their cognitive ability merits. Teachers should consider whether the language of the written text is necessary to achieving the learning outcomes or if the text and task could be presented in a different way. Two such examples are now presented with a discussion of the textual difficulties and some solutions.

The first example is from a science text (Ginn 1990: 16):

If you took a same-sized piece of wood from all the different trees in the world, the heaviest wood would be the black ironwood from South Africa. It is even heavier than *lignum vitae* which was used for centuries to make hard-wearing pulleys and bowls . . . If Noah's Ark really existed then it would hold the record for being the longest wooden ship . . . The biggest tree in the world is called General Sherman.

The intended learning outcomes

The purpose of this text is to stimulate pupils' interest and help them to find out more about the science topic under consideration (wood). There are no specific tasks within the book, although there are a few suggestions for experiments. The book is likely to be used as an information text during a science topic. The facts and figures are interesting and it would be a useful text for pupils to create reports on different materials.

The potential difficulties of the text for bilingual pupils and possible solutions

The syntax of the text is complex and some of the vocabulary is confusing – it may be tempting to suggest that the bilingual pupil is not given this text. The danger with this is that the child will not have the opportunity in class to develop from basic language (BICS) to using the more academic language (CALP) required for success. If the other children in the class regularly use the text, the teacher needs to consider how to help the bilingual pupil to also use the text.

The first two sentences present facts about the names, sources and uses of the heaviest woods in the world. This would be easier to read in a tabular form:

names of wood in order of weight	found in	uses
black ironwood	South Africa	
lignum vitae		pulleys and bowls

In order to help the bilingual child to access the text, the teacher could devise a paired activity which requires the pair to read the text and complete the table. After a few sessions of working collaboratively to access the text, the bilingual pupil will be better enabled to understand the complex sentence structures in this and other similar texts. In this way the classroom teacher is helping the child to develop cognitive academic language proficiency.

If Noah's Ark really existed then it would hold the record for being the longest wooden ship. This sentence contains linguistic and cultural difficulties. Unless the child is a Christian who has a knowledge of the Old Testament, the reference to Noah's Ark will be meaningless. The conditional tense is very complex and it is hard to understand the meaning implied by the sentence. If the teacher establishes pairs of reading partners in the classroom, these pairs can ask each other questions of the text when there is unfamiliar vocabulary or concepts.

The teacher should note for long-term planning that the child may need opportunities to read, hear and practise the function of speculating, using conditional tense structures.

The biggest tree in the world is called General Sherman. The rest of the discussion about trees has given the botanical or common name for them (black ironwood, *lignum vitae*). It is difficult to understand that General Sherman is not the name of a type of tree, but a specific name given to a specific tree. This will need to be explained to many of the children, not just the bilingual child. The teacher could model questions which will lead to speculation, thus meeting the assessed needs of the bilingual pupils which were identified earlier in this discussion, for example, *Why might the biggest tree be called General Sherman? What might you call a tree if it was the widest/smallest/leafiest tree in the world?*

Mathematics textbooks frequently use a considerable amount of language to explain a mathematical problem, often in an attempt to add context to the problem. This example is from a maths textbook for children working at National Curriculum Levels 2–3/5–14 Level B (Heinemann 1992: 9):

> 4 (a) 97 children went to the Trail Take Away in the morning. 78 went in the afternoon.
> What is the difference in the number of children?
> (b) The cook fried 30 fish. He had orders for 42 fish. How many more did he need to fry?
> 5 Write a story about the Trail Take Away for 19 − 6 = 13.

The intentions of this textbook task are to give contextualised opportunities for children to perform subtraction sums and to recognise the different ways of expressing a subtraction sum.

In addition to subtraction skills however, a range of English language skills is needed if the pupil is to succeed. The pupil needs to be able to read, understand and organise the text to find the actual sum required. In order to respond to question 5, the pupil needs to be able to construct a mathematical problem in sentences, using the contextual language of the Take Away.

The previous questions on the page are recorded as subtraction problems without the context, e.g.

76
− 31 or Write these using − and = 35 minus 4 is 31.
‾‾‾

By completing these numerical tasks correctly, the child can demonstrate the intended learning and it may not be necessary for the child to also answer questions 4 and 5 above. As with the science text however, it is important that the child is not always told to ignore the word tasks as these skills will be required. The teacher will need to plan time to teach the bilingual child how to understand the language surrounding maths problems. This may be a task that the EAL teacher, having specialist language knowledge, could address.

In general, in order to assess curriculum materials for bilingual learners, the teacher needs to ask a number of questions of the text. These are presented in the photocopiable format at the end of the chapter.

'What should be in a school policy for bilingual learners?'

The need for a school policy for the education of bilingual learners has been mentioned at several points throughout this book and I shall now suggest some of the important areas which should be included in such a policy. This discussion will not provide a finite answer to policy content, as every school works in a different context, with different numbers of bilingual children and different resources. However, there are some important factors that need to be considered in any school policy for bilingual learners. The discussion will be summarised at the end of the chapter with a photocopiable format which can be used as a starting point for school INSET towards the development of a policy.

The first factor to consider is that for the policy to be any more than simply a piece of paper, the school community needs to feel ownership of the policy. Therefore the policy should be drafted by a working group which includes not only teaching staff, but also ancillary staff, parents and pupils. Policy-making should be preceded by working group meetings to discuss the meaning and value of bilingualism. This can then lead to a statement about bilingual learners and bilingualism which will be a foundation for the whole policy.

Such a statement might include a definition of the bilingual learner, a statement which values the languages of all children and their families in school and a recognition of the distinction between language support for bilingual pupils and learning support. It is important to include in the policy a means of monitoring the language use of pupils in the school, using, for example, the format for recording children's language use from Chapter 1. The policy will also need to identify who is responsible for maintaining these records.

The policy for the education of bilingual pupils must be related to the school's anti-racist policy. Many bilingual pupils encounter racism in their daily lives and this has a negative impact on their learning. The policy should state where the procedures for dealing with racist incidents are to be found. It may be that, in the course of devising a school policy for the education of bilingual learners, the school's anti-racist policy should be revised.

It is essential that consideration is given to how the policy will be monitored and reviewed and who will have responsibility for this. The training needs of new and temporary staff should be identified and a plan drawn up for ongoing training of existing staff.

Three further areas which have been addressed throughout this book need specific consideration in the policy if education for bilingual learners is to be effective: home–school contact, teaching practices and assessment. As discussed in Chapter 3, school liaison with parents is essential. The policy must state the importance of parents maintaining the home language, and should also address issues around communication with bilingual parents, access to meetings with teachers and how parents can support their children's learning.

In order to implement best practice for bilingual learners, the policy needs to make statements about teaching which will support teachers to develop collaborative tasks and to plan language support for their bilingual pupils across the curriculum. Resources such as dual language textbooks, collaborative games and artifacts which reflect the cultural diversity of the school should be considered. The policy also needs to make statements about the role(s) of the EAL/EMAG/bilingual support teacher(s) and how the school will enable liaison between them and the mainstream teachers for the benefit of the bilingual pupils.

Assessment statements in the policy require to assert that assessment acknowledges the child's bilingualism. Where possible, the child's oral and literacy skills in the first language should be assessed. Recorded assessments must acknowledge the child's development of English language skills across the curriculum, indicating strengths and areas which will need attention.

There will be other issues for consideration in school policies dependent on, for example, the existence of centralised education authority policies, resources and personnel, and links with associated schools. The format which follows should, however, provide guidance for schools wishing to start a discussion on policy for bilingual learners.

Planning collaborative tasks

Name of bilingual pupil _____

Curricular area/lesson title _____

Task description

How many pupils in group?

Role of bilingual pupil?

Roles of other pupils?

Functions of language	Structures of language

Assessing curriculum materials for bilingual learners

- Name of resource _____

- What is/are the intended learning outcome(s) of using this material?

  _____

  _____

- What English language skills does the pupil need in order to demonstrate the learning in this way?

  _____

  _____

- What might be some of the difficulties encountered by the bilingual pupils with this material?

- e.g. vocabulary, _____

- complex sentences, _____

- lack of clarity in instructions _____

- Can the learning be demonstrated in another way?

- e.g. listen and oral response rather than read and write _____

- notes in a writing frame rather than continuous prose _____

- other _____

Other teacher or pupil action required?

  _____

Towards a school policy for the education of bilingual learners: questions for consideration

Who should be in the policy working group?

School statement on bilingualism and bilingual learners.

Who will be responsible for monitoring and reviewing the implementation of the policy?

Who will be responsible for monitoring languages used in the school and how will this information be collected?

School statement on anti-racist education and dealing with racist incidents.

How will training support on the implementation of the policy be provided for new staff?

Issues to consider in home–school liaison:
  encouraging parents to support development of home language

  curriculum support

  homework

  translation of written communication

  access for parents to teachers

  provision of interpreters

  parental support for school learning

Issues to consider in teaching:

statement concerning distinction between language support and learning support

statement concerning the planning of language support for bilingual learners by a consideration of the language necessary for the learning

role of EAL/bilingual support teacher(s)

liaison between mainstream class/subject teachers and EAL/bilingual support teacher(s)

statement concerning value of collaborative learning

text resources

culturally relevant resources

Issues to consider in assessment:

assessment to take account of child being bilingual

assessment in the child's first language

assessment of English language development across the curriculum

Useful Addresses and Websites

Useful addresses

Collaborative Learning Project
Stuart Scott
17 Barford Street
London, N1 0QB
Tel: 020 7226 8885
Email: *collearn@rmplc.co.uk*
www.collaborativelearning.org

This project organises a swapshop of materials developed by teachers for use in collaborative group work across the curriculum. Samples are available on the website.

Commission for Racial Equality
Elliot House
10/12 Allington Street
London, SW1E 5EH
Tel: 020 7828 7022
www.cre.gov.uk

DfES Publications
PO Box 5050
Sherwood Park
Annesley
Nottingham, NG15 0DJ
Tel: 0845 602 2260
www.dfes.gov.uk/index.htm

Many useful materials, particularly *The Learning Journey,* a guide to the National Curriculum for parents available in a range of community languages.

Mantra Publishing
5 Alexandra Grove
London, N12 8NU
Tel: 020 8445 5123
Email: *info@mantrapublishing.com*
www.mantrapublishing.com

Publishes dual language books and multilingual posters and videos.

NALDIC: National Association for Language Development in the Curriculum
c/o Helen Abji, secretary
Luton Learning Resource Centre
Strangers Way
Luton, LU3 5NS
Email: *abjih@luton.gov.uk*
www.naldic.org.uk

NALDIC publishes a series of very useful booklets on best practice for bilingual pupils. The association also organises an annual conference with prestigious speakers.

Oxfam Development Education
4th floor, 4 Bridge Place
London, SW1V 1XY
Tel: 020 7931 7660
Email: *vicdeved@oxfam.org.uk*
www.oxfam.org.uk/coolplanet

A catalogue of very useful resources is available from Oxfam. The website has a super range of resources to help address the concept of global citizenship.

Refugee Council
Publications Unit
3 Bondway
London, SW1 1SJ
Tel: 020 7820 3000
Email: *refcounciluk@gn.apc.prg*
www.refugeecouncil.org.uk
Excellent educational materials for use in schools, including free booklet *Helping Refugee Children in Schools* and illustrated word lists for use with newly arrived pupils in a range of languages.

Runnymede Trust
Suite 106
The London Fruit and Wool Exchange
London, E1 6EP
Tel: 020 7377 9222
www.runnymedetrust.org.uk

Many useful discussions on the website of this organisation which aims to challenge racial discrimination and influence anti-racist legislation.

Save the Children UK
17 Grove Lane
London, SE5 8RD
Tel: 020 7703 5400
www.savethechildren.org.uk

Produces many useful resources and reports, including resources on working with refugee children.

SATEAL: Scottish Association for Teaching English as an Additional Language
c/o EDEALS
Castlehill Primary School
Rosslyn Road
Bearsden, G12 4DL
Email: *secretary@sateal.org.uk*
www.sateal.org.uk

The association organises an annual conference in the spring and co-organises the annual TESOL (Scotland) conference in the autumn.

Useful websites

Theory

Jim Cummins' ESL/L2 web page
http://www.iteachilearn.com/cummins/

Debates

National Clearing House for English Language Acquisition
(US-based discussion list)
http://www.ncela.gwu.edu/
National Association for Bilingual Education
(US-based discussion list)
http://www.nabe.org/

University of Birmingham School of Education Bilingualism Database
(UK-based information list)
http://www.edu.bham.ac.uk//bilingualism/database/dbase.htm

Hampshire education authority bilingual support service provides web-based
information on many of the languages and cultures of children at school in Britain.
This site also has interesting comparisons between the grammar of English and
other community languages.
http://www.hants.gov.uk/blss/advice/lcr/home.htm

Resources

Helpful for suggested strategies to support bilingual pupils:
Collaborative Learning Project (see Useful addresses section)
http://www.collaborativelearning.org/

The EAL subject specialist page of the TES site is particularly useful for mainstream teachers featuring ideas for those with limited experience of EAL learners
through features such as 'Good practice tips for teachers of EAL pupils'.
http://www.tes.co.uk/your_subject/subject_index.asp?subject=EAL

An online catalogue is available from Bilingual Supplies for Children which
includes single and dual language books, multilingual stickers and language games.
http://www.bilingual-books.com

A link to a vast range of multilingual computer resources, such as overlays and
translators is available at this website *http://www.gy.com*
    On first sight it does not look like you have reached the correct site, but follow
the links to multilingual computer resources.

Newspapers

Helpful for searching for recent debates on the education of bilingual learners and refugee pupils in the UK.
http://www.guardian.co.uk/
http://www.observer.co.uk/

In addition to the books referred to in the Bibliography, the following texts offer valuable resources and advice to teachers of bilingual pupils.

Edwards, V. (1996) *The Other Languages: A Guide to Multilingual Classrooms.* Reading: Reading and Language Information Centre.
Multilingual Resources for Children Project (1995) *Building Bridges: Multilingual Resources for Children.* Clevedon: Multilingual Matters.

Bibliography

Archibald, A. (1994) *Bilingualism and Special Education.* Unpublished report. Central Region Education Department.

Arshad, R., Closs, A. and Stead, J. (1999) *Doing our Best Scottish School Education, Refugee Pupils and Parents: A Strategy for Social Inclusion.* Summary report of a two year research study on the school experience of refugee pupils in Scotland. Edinburgh: CERES.

Baetens-Beardsmore, H. (1982) *Bilingualism: Basic Principles.* Clevedon: Multilingual Matters.

Baetens-Beardsmore, H. (ed.) (1993) *European Models of Bilingual Education.* Clevedon: Multilingual Matters.

Baker, C. (1996) *Foundations of Bilingual Education and Bilingualism* (2nd edn). Clevedon: Multilingual Matters.

Biggs, A.P. and Edwards, V. (1994) 'I treat them all the same: teacher–pupil talk in multiethnic classrooms', in Graddol, D., Maybin, J. and Stierer, B. (eds) *Researching Language and Literacy in a Social Context.* Clevedon: Multilingual Matters.

Blackledge, A. (2000) *Literacy, Power and Social Justice.* Stoke-on-Trent: Trentham Books.

Bourne, J. (1990) 'Local authority provision for bilingual pupils', *Educational Research* 32(1), 3–13.

Bourne, J. (1997) 'The continuing revolution: teaching as learning in the mainstream multilingual classroom', in Leung, C. and Cable, C. (eds) *English as an Additional Language: Changing Perspectives.* Watford: National Association for Language Development in the Curriculum (NALDIC).

Brandt, G. (1986) *The Realisation of Anti-Racist Teaching.* London: Falmer Press.

Brittan, E. (1976) 'Multiracial education 2: teacher opinion on aspects of school life', *Educational Research* 18(2), 96–107.

Cazden, C.B. and Snow, C.E. (1990) *English Plus: Issues in Bilingual Education.* London: Sage.

Closs, A., Stead, J. and Arshad, R. (1999) *The School Experience of Refugee Children in Scotland: Report of a Two Year Research Study.* Edinburgh: Moray House Institute of Education.

Commission for Racial Equality (CRE) (1986) *Teaching English as a Second Language: Calderdale LEA.* The Calderdale Report. London: CRE.

Commission for Racial Equality (CRE) (1996) *Special Educational Need Assessment in Strathclyde: Report of a Formal Investigation.* London: CRE.

Constantino, R. (1994) 'A study concerning instruction of ESL students comparing all English classroom teacher knowledge and English as a Second Language teacher knowledge', *Journal of Educational Issues of Language Minority Students* 13, 37–57.

Cummins, J. (1979) 'Cognitive/academic language proficiency, linguistic interdependence, the optimum age question and some other matters', *Working Papers on Bilingualism* 19, 121–9.

Cummins, J. (1984) *Bilingualism and Special Education: Issues in Assessment and Pedagogy.* Clevedon: Multilingual Matters.

Cummins, J. (1986) 'Empowering minority students: a framework for intervention', *Harvard Educational Review* 56(1), 18–36.

Cummins, J. (1996) *Negotiating Identities: Education for Empowerment in a Diverse Society.* Los Angeles, CA: California Association for Bilingual Education (CABE).

Cummins, J. (2000) 'Putting language proficiency in its place: responding to critiques of the conversational/academic language distinction', in Cenoz, J. and Jessner, U. (eds) *English in Europe: The Acquisition of a Third Language.* Clevedon: Multilingual Matters.

Cummins, J. and Swain, M. (1986) *Bilingualism in Education: Aspects of Theory, Research and Practice.* London: Longman.

Department for Education and Employment (DfEE) (1998) *Making the Difference: Teaching and Learning Strategies in Successful Multi-Ethnic Schools.* London: DfEE.

Department for Education and Employment (DfEE) (2000) *Removing the Barriers: Raising Achievement Levels for Minority Ethnic Pupils.* London: DfEE.

Department of Education and Science (DES) (1963) *English for Immigrants.* London: DES.

Department of Education and Science (DES) (1975) *A Language for Life.* The Bullock Report. London: HMSO.

Department of Education and Science (DES) (1985) *Education for All.* The Swann Report. London: HMSO.

Department of Education and Science (DES) (1989) *English for Ages 5-16.* The Cox Report. London: HMSO.

Department of Education and Science (DES) (1990) *Modern Foreign Languages for Ages 11–16.* The Harris Report. London: HMSO.

Dhondy, F. (1981) 'Teaching young Blacks', in James, A. and Jeffcoate, R. (eds) *The School in the Multicultural Society*. London: Harper and Row.

Ellis, R. (1985) *Understanding Second Language Acquisition*. Oxford: Oxford University Press.

Fishman, J.A. (1976) *Bilingual Education: An International Sociological Perspective*. Rowley, MA: Newbury House.

Gee, J.P. (1999) *An Introduction to Discourse Analysis: Theory and Method*. London: Routledge.

Gibbons, P. (1991) *Learning to Learn in a Second Language*. Newtown, Australia: PETA.

Gillborn, D. and Gipps, C. (1996) *Recent Research on the Achievements of Ethnic Minority Pupils*. London: HMSO.

Ginn (1990) *Ginn Science Level 5: Wood and Paper*. Aylesbury: Ginn.

Gonzales, J.M. (1975) 'Coming of age in bilingual/bicultural education', *Inequality in Education* 19, 5–17.

Graves, D. (1983) *Writing: Teachers and Children at Work*. London: Heinemann.

Gregory, E. (ed.) (1997) *One Child, Many Worlds: Early Learning in Multicultural Communities*. London: David Fulton Publishers.

Hall, D. (2002) *Assessing the Needs of Bilingual Pupils*. London: David Fulton Publishers.

Heath, S.B. (1983) *Ways with Words*. Cambridge: Cambridge University Press.

Heinemann (1992) *Heinemann Maths 3 Textbook*. Oxford: Heinemann.

Herriman, M. and Burnaby, B. (eds) (1996) *Language Policies in English-Dominant Countries*. Clevedon: Multilingual Matters.

Holmes McDougall (1986) *Link-Up 3a*. Edinburgh: Holmes McDougall.

Kaplan, R.B. and Baldauf, R.B., Jnr. (1997) *Language Planning from Practice to Theory*. Clevedon: Multilingual Matters.

Kenner, C. (1997) 'A child writes from her everyday world: using home texts to develop biliteracy at school', in Gregory, E. (ed.) *One Child, Many Worlds: Early Learning in Multicultural Communities*. London: David Fulton Publishers.

Kenner, C. (1999) *Home Pages: Literacy Links for Bilingual Children*. Stoke-on-Trent: Trentham Books.

Krashen, S. (1982) *Principles and Practice of Second Language Acquisition*. Oxford: Pergamon Press.

Learning and Teaching Scotland (LTS) (2000) *Education for Citizenship*. Consultation paper. Edinburgh: LTS.

Leung, C. (1996) *Linguistic Diversity in the 1990s: Some Language Education Issues for Minority Ethnic Pupils*. Watford: National Association for Language Development in the Curriculum (NALDIC).

Lucas, T., Henze, R. and Donato, R. (1990) 'Promoting the success of Latino language minority students: an exploratory study of six high schools', *Harvard Educational Review* 60, 315–40.

Luthar, O., McLeod, K. and Zagar, M. (eds) (2001) *Liberal Democracy, Citizenship and Education*. Oakville, Ontario: Mosaic Press.

Mackey, W.F. (1970) 'A typology of bilingual education', *Foreign Language Annals* 3, 596–608.

Malave, L.M. and Duquette, G. (eds) (1991) *Language, Culture and Cognition*. Clevedon: Multilingual Matters.

Mills, R.W and Mills, J. (1993) *Bilingualism in the Primary School*. London: Routledge.

Morgan, E. (1996) *Collected Translations*. Manchester: Carcanet Press.

Oxfam (1997) *A Curriculum for Global Citizenship*. Oxford: Oxfam.

Powney, J., McPake, J., Hall, S. and Lyall, L. (1998) *Education of Minority Ethnic Groups in Scotland: A Review of Research*. Edinburgh: Scottish Council for Research in Education.

Qualifications and Curriculum Authority (QCA) (1998) *Education for Citizenship and the Teaching of Democracy in Schools*. Final report of the Advisory Group on Citizenship. London: QCA.

Qualifications and Curriculum Authority (QCA) (2000) *A Language in Common: Assessing English as an Additional Language*. London: QCA.

Rattansi, A. (1992) 'Changing the subject? Racism, culture and education', in Donald, J. and Rattansi, A. (eds) *'Race', Culture and Difference*. London: Sage.

Rutter, J. (1998) *Refugees: A Resource Book for Primary Schools*. London: Refugee Council.

Scottish Consultative Council on the Curriculum (SCCC) (1994) *Languages for Life*. Dundee: SCCC.

Scottish Office Education Department (SOED) (1991) *English Language 5–14*. Edinburgh: SOED.

Siraj-Blatchford, I. (1994) *The Early Years: Laying the Foundation for Racial Equality*. Stoke-on-Trent: Trentham Books.

Skutnabb-Kangas, T. (1981) *Bilingualism or Not: The Education of Minorities*. Clevedon: Multilingual Matters.

Smyth, G. (2001a) '"I feel this challenge – but I don't have the background". Teachers' responses to their bilingual pupils in 6 Scottish primary schools: an ethnographic study'. Unpublished thesis, Open University.

Smyth, G. (2001b) 'Theoretical approaches to multicultural education from a British perspective', in Luthar, O., McLeod, K. and Zagar, M. (eds) *Liberal Democracy, Citizenship and Education*. Oakville, Ontario: Mosaic Press.

Smyth, G. and McKee, T. (1997) 'Multicultural anti-racist education policy in two teacher education institutions', in *Association for Teacher Education in Europe (ATEE) Conference Papers*, 184–91. Glasgow: University of Strathclyde.

Stubbs, M. (1994) 'Educational language planning in England and Wales: multi-cultural rhetoric and assimilationist assumptions', in Maybin, J. (ed.) *Language and Literacy in Social Practice*. Clevedon: Multilingual Matters.

Styles, M. (1989) *Collaboration and Writing*. Milton Keynes: Open University Press.

Taylor, D. (1983) *Family Literacy*. London: Heinemann.

Teacher Training Agency (TTA) (2000) *Raising the Attainment of Minority Ethnic Pupils*. London: TTA.

Thomas, W.P. and Collier, V. (1997) *School Effectiveness for Language Minority Students*. Washington, DC: National Clearing House for Bilingual Education (NCBE).

Thompson, L., Fleming, M. and Byram, M. (1996) 'Languages and language policy in Britain', in Herriman, M. and Burnaby, B. (eds) *Language Policies in English-Dominant Countries*. Clevedon: Multilingual Matters.

Troyna, B. and Williams, J. (1986) *Racism, Education and the State*. Beckenham: Croom Helm.

Verma, M.K., Corrigan, K.P. and Firth, S. (1995) *Working with Bilingual Children*. Clevedon: Multilingual Matters.

Wiles, S. (1985) 'Language and learning in multi-ethnic classrooms: strategies for supporting bilingual students', in Wells, G. and Nicholls, J. (eds) *Language and Learning: An Interactional Perspective*. Lewes: Falmer Press.

Young, M. (with Commins, E.) (2002) *Global Citizenship: The Handbook for Primary Teaching*. Cambridge: Chris Kington Publishing; Oxford: Oxfam.

Name Index

Subject Index